Generating Buy-In

Generating Buy-In

Mastering the Language of Leadership

MARK S. WALTON

Foreword by

William Ury, Harvard Law School
Best-Selling Co-Author, *Getting to Yes*

AMACOM

American Management Association

New York • Atlanta • Brussels • Chicago • Mexico City • San Francisco
Shanghai • Tokyo • Toronto • Washington, D.C.

Special discounts on bulk quantities of AMACOM books are available to corporations, professional associations, and other organizations. For details, contact Special Sales Department, AMACOM, a division of American Management Association, 1601 Broadway, New York, NY 10019.
Tel.: 212-903-8316. Fax: 212-903-8083.
Web site: www.amacombooks.org

This publication is designed to provide accurate and authoritative information in regard to the subject matter covered. It is sold with the understanding that the publisher is not engaged in rendering legal, accounting, or other professional service. If legal advice or other expert assistance is required, the services of a competent professional person should be sought.

Library of Congress Cataloging-in-Publication Data

Walton, Mark S., 1950–
    Generating buy-in : mastering the language of leadership / Mark S. Walton ; foreword by William Ury.
        p.   cm.
    ISBN 0-8144-0905-9
    1. Communication in management.   2. Leadership.   3. Persuasion (Psychology)   I. Title.
HD30.3.W35   2004
658.4'5—dc21   2003011093

Printing number

10 9 8 7 6 5 4 3 2 1

For my parents, Marjorie and Sidney Walton, who shared with me their love of books.

Contents

Foreword

by William Ury, Ph.D.
Associate Director, Program on Negotiation, Harvard Law School
Co-Author, *Getting to Yes*

I first met Mark Walton in 1990 when he was a senior correspondent and anchorman at CNN. With war games filling the airwaves in the wake of Saddam Hussein's invasion of Kuwait, Mark and I collaborated on a primetime television peace game, a simulation of a negotiation designed to resolve the crisis diplomatically. I found myself impressed by Mark's communication savvy, his creativity, and his willingness to take risks and try new approaches. His years of experience as a network journalist, covering the White House, politics, and business, were clearly evident.

When Mark left CNN several years later, I was one of those who encouraged him strongly to draw on his rich background to help others learn how to communicate more effectively. He took up the challenge and this book is one of the exceptional results.

Generating Buy-In could not address a more important competence for executives, indeed for anyone who hopes to lead, influence, and persuade others. We are living in an era that might be called the Negotiation Revolution. Traditionally, decisions were made by the boss at the top of a vertical pyramid. Nowadays, in order to get their jobs done, people depend on dozens of individuals and organizations over whom they exercise no direct control. They cannot impose a decision; they are compelled to negotiate.

Even in the military, the epitome of a pyramidal organization, where people are accustomed to giving orders and receiving instant obedience, the new reality applies. I found myself surprised once, while on a lecture tour in Colombia, to receive a request from the Chief of the Armed Forces to give a talk to his generals and admirals. They required negotiating skills, he explained, in order to obtain the budget they sought from politicians, the cease fires they wanted from guerrilla leaders, and the cooperation they needed from their peers. Even with direct subordinates, he added, they could not get the kind of performance they wanted by simple orders; they needed to negotiate for it. In Mark Walton's language, they needed to get "buy-in."

Based on his extensive experience in the media, the military, politics, and business, as well as his in-depth research into the dynamics of influence in fields as varied as government, sales and marketing, advertising, and courtroom law, Mark has derived a very simple, yet uniquely-powerful formula for effective persuasion. It entails telling a positive strategic story and, on that basis, asking your audience for a specific commitment to action. As in negotiation, the key to success lies in understanding the basic needs and motivations of your audience.

Indeed, the formula is so simple that readers may think, "But I knew that already." And so we do in a sense. While the basic idea is indeed common sense, it can be described more accurately as "uncommon sense," in other words, common sense uncommonly practiced. By codifying it in simple memorable language and providing a practical framework and inspiring examples, Mark gives us the tools to make this approach work every day for our benefit and that of others.

Mark has certainly won my "buy-in." I can think of many uses for this approach in my own field of negotiation, whether it is persuading the parties to come to terms, or figuring out how leaders can persuade their constituencies about the merits of an agreement.

You do not need, however, to be a political leader or a corporate executive; anyone interested in influencing fellow human beings can benefit from this book's wise and practical advice. It's a keeper!

William Ury
Boulder, Colorado
March, 2003

Acknowledgments

If we are truly fortunate, the universe will provide, at just the right times and places, soul mates who will nurture, support, challenge, and inspire us to take the leaps that are essential to discovering and creating our right livelihood.

In working with me to build the Center for Leadership Communication and to make this book a reality, my wife and number one soul mate, Jane, tirelessly assumed the role of chief encourager, editor, scheduler, protector, detailer, and brain trust. During our decades together, I have come to see that true love means never, ever being able to adequately say thank you. I shall forever aspire to give her back the "gift" that she is.

When I was in search of a new avenue of self-expression, my friend and soul mate, Bill Ury, showed me a whole new city of lights in the world of executive consulting and education. If there's such a thing as an angel, Bill is it. His contribution to my thinking, my work, and to this book is simply incalculable. Years ago, Bill taught me that "IOUs are what makes the world go 'round." I owe him several planetary revolutions.

In my work, I have been fortunate to meet and collaborate with a great number of colleagues, friends, and clients. Each, in her or his own way, has been a source of insights that have helped shape this book.

I am particularly appreciative of the efforts of a special few— Ron Kirkpatrick, Linda Koffenberger, Dan Mangelsdorf, Frank

Morgan, Susan Palmer, and my old friend Walt Riker—all of whom generously gave of their time and energy to review early drafts and provide invaluable guidance.

I owe a similar debt of gratitude to Andy Ambraziejus and the production team at AMACOM books, and especially to my editor, Adrienne Hickey, for seeing the possibilities in *Generating Buy-In* and bringing them to life.

Mark Walton
Chapel Hill, North Carolina

Introduction

We All Need Somebody's Buy-In

Public sentiment is everything. With public sentiment, nothing can fail; without it, nothing can succeed.

—Abraham Lincoln

However well-positioned, intelligent, or accomplished we are, to succeed in this twenty-first century, we all need somebody's buy-in.

The President of the United States appears before Congress to generate support for a war on terrorism. A CEO goes to Wall Street to rebuild confidence in his company. You present your proposal to the board. A division VP launches a new product. A regional sales director seeks to motivate her team. You have dinner with a major client, a reporter, or speak to an industry group.

Other people's buy-in—*their understanding, commitment, and action in support of our goals*—has always been enormously important. But in today's world, it has become the most valuable asset of all. And the ability to influence people's thoughts and feelings, to generate their buy-in, has emerged as *the* paramount leadership skill.

Why? In the twenty-first-century workplace and marketplace, the dynamics of power, authority, and credibility have radically changed. *No matter who you are or where you work,*

people no longer need to follow your lead, buy what you sell, or ac-
cept what you say. What's more, they're increasingly unlikely to do
so, with each passing day.

The workplace has become a "free agent nation," its citizens an all-volunteer force. Command-and-control management and unquestioned loyalty are ideas whose time has come and gone. In the new organizational world, "there's nothing you can force people to do," says Dow Chemical chairman Bill Stavropoulos. *"Now, people have to believe, and they have to believe in you."*[1]

Today's marketplace is a free-for-all, moving in Internet time. Companies, competitors, and offerings glom together in an undifferentiated blur. Investors, customers, and clients click, scan, blink, and decide. Never have they had more options, or fewer clear incentives, to send their business your way.

In the twenty-first century, to refresh Abraham Lincoln's observation at the beginning of this Introduction, *buy-in is everything*. With it, nothing can fail; without it, nothing can succeed. Not ideas, organizations, products, or services. Not you or me.

The Power You Will Gain

This book provides you with a uniquely powerful communication methodology—*a language of buy-in and leadership*—built for success in today's formidable, fast-forward environment.

Whatever your buy-in challenges, *this language will empower* you to produce the results you want and need with greater ease, speed, and effectiveness. It can be applied in every situation, and in every medium—spoken or written—in which you communicate. You can use it in important presentations and speeches, one-on-one conversations, high-pressure meetings, media interviews, or events. With this language you can write proposals, letters, memos, or e-mails.

It is a synergy of ancient wisdom and state-of-the-art communication strategy that will give you a significant edge in an extremely competitive twenty-first-century world.

As a network news correspondent, strategist, and executive educator, I've witnessed its practical potency, again and again, pulsing like a fundamental rhythm through the communications of the world-class leaders, managers, and masterful marketers I've had the opportunity to work with and observe up-close.

In the pages ahead, their secret for generating buy-in will become yours. You will see how leading executives—from Presidents Ronald Reagan and George W. Bush to General Electric's Jack Welch—and highly-successful organizations—from Coca-Cola and Intel to the U.S. Army—have used this language to achieve their most important strategic objectives.

Through these and other real-world examples, behind-the-scenes interviews, and practical exercises, you will learn a powerful step-by-step process for targeting your audience's needs, capturing their attention, and communicating in a positive, memorable way—without hard-selling or manipulating—to successfully:

- Build, lead, and manage organizations

- Motivate individuals, groups, and teams

- Market ideas, products, and services

- Gain the commitment and loyalty of customers

- Generate support from analysts, investors, and regulators

- Win elections and legislative approval

- Turn crises into positive, value-added outcomes

A Guide to Mastering Buy-In

For all of its impact, I am confident that you will find this *language of buy-in* surprisingly straightforward, even easy to learn and apply.

I say this because I share this methodology with hundreds of executives, each year, in corporate, military, government, and graduate business school workshops around the world. And overwhelmingly, their feedback reads like this, from a Fortune 100 senior manager:

> I have read many books and taken courses in communication, negotiation, and leadership and nothing has worked as well for me as your *simple* approach. You may be describing something that great leaders have known, but before you showed it to me, no one else had, and I hadn't figured it out on my own. What you taught me was truly an Aha!

For the many talented executives with whom I've worked, and for those of you I've yet to have the pleasure of meeting, this book is designed as a guide to mastery of a remarkable technology for leadership in the workplace *and* marketplace of the twenty-first century.

May it provide you a powerful breakthrough in generating buy-in!

Generating Buy-In

PART ONE

Understanding the Language of Buy-In

CHAPTER 1

What Triggers Buy-In?

I will bring you up out of the affliction . . . unto a land
flowing with milk and honey.

—Exodus 3:17

Settle back in your television chair tonight, remote control in hand, and in the matter of a few short hours, an economy larger than the GNP of many small countries will pass before your eyes.

Between blinks, millions of dollars in commercial stories will flicker in and out of your consciousness. If you're watching a top-rated program, like the Super Bowl, sponsors may have spent more than $3 million, in time and production costs, to get a thirty-second shot at your mind.

Say "good evening" to the greatest technology of influence in history, one that is dedicated to a singular strategic objective: getting your attention, interest, and buy-in, and that of every human being, worldwide, within its line-of-sight.

You can be certain that, not for one second or cent, are the masters of the television universe fooling around. Whether they're seeking buy-in for automobiles, clothes, investments, or vacations, they will program their technology to communicate with you and me in the most compelling language ever found.

They will speak to us in strategic stories night after day after night. These are stories that are strategically designed to project a positive future.

TV people did not invent this language. But they have mastered, updated, and capitalized on it in a huge way. So have successful leaders, managers, and professionals throughout the ages. The reason?

Strategic stories of a positive future have been the most powerful language of buy-in since, if not before, the beginning of recorded time.

Let me show you why.

A Perfect Summer Afternoon

Relax for a moment and do a brief thought experiment with me. I know you'll enjoy it and discover something of great value.

Consider this short phrase:

A perfect summer afternoon

Roll the words over a couple of times.

A perfect summer afternoon. What comes to mind? Where are you on this perfect summer afternoon? Who are you with? What are you doing? *A perfect summer afternoon.* What's the temperature? How do you feel? Are there any sounds on your perfect summer afternoon? Any tastes or smells? *A perfect summer afternoon.* Fast-forward the scene a couple of hours. What's going on now? Or now?

When I conduct this experiment in my executive workshops, most folks are ready to put on their shorts or bathing suits. They report experiencing themselves everywhere from mountain resorts to the Mediterranean coast. They're swimming, playing golf, reading, enjoying their favorite food and beverages. Some are with their wives, husbands, and kids. Some are doing other things with . . . well, other folks.

How about you? *A perfect summer afternoon.* If you actually take a moment to reflect on these words, you'll have an opportunity to examine the inner mechanism of your and every human mind. And you'll arrive at a significant finding:

> WE "THINK" IN *STORIES*. STORIES, FILLED WITH PICTURES—
> IMAGES OF LIFE—ARE LITERALLY THE LANGUAGE,
> THE CURRENCY OF OUR MINDS.

Aristotle Knew: Stories Trigger Buy-In

"It is impossible even to think without a mental picture," said Aristotle in his essay, *On Memory and Recollection*, in A.D. 450.

Aristotle and countless other thinkers have pointed out that the human mind is like a private screening room, continually rolling complex mental stories that have an uncanny power to soothe, scare, interest, or stimulate us.

Our memories, for example, are all stories. They're stories filled with pictures, sounds, and feelings. Think: senior year in high school. Who do you see? What's going on? What emotions are you experiencing?

The same thing occurs when we're asleep. What we call dreaming, according to cognitive psychologists, is an automatic phenomenon that begins in healthy babies long before they can speak. When it shows up later, in school, or when we're bored stiff in business meetings, we label it daydreaming! It's all the same stuff.

Now, if the mind "thinks" this way, what might we conclude about the most effective way to influence that mind? Of course. *The most effective way to influence the human mind is to communicate with it in its basic programming language: a story.*

And, if our objective is to trigger buy-in from people, for a change, proposal, idea, or, perhaps, a product that will impact their future, what kind of a story is most likely to succeed? Now you've got it.

THE AGE-OLD SECRET TO GENERATING BUY-IN IS TO STRATEGICALLY DESIGN, TARGET, AND DELIVER A STORY THAT PROJECTS A *POSITIVE FUTURE.*

CHAPTER 2

Every Leader Tells a Story

Look at Winston Churchill and Franklin Roosevelt.
They said: This is what it's going to be.

—John F. Welch, Jr.
Former Chairman and CEO
General Electric Corporation

A winter sunbeam warmed the North Portico of 1600 Pennsylvania Avenue the moment Ronald Reagan's motorcade arrived. As CNN's chief White House correspondent, I watched President Jimmy Carter step forward to greet the man who had defeated him resoundingly in the 1980 campaign and who, within hours, would replace him in office.

It was January 20, 1981. America's unemployment rate stood at 7 percent, inflation was mounting at 12 percent, gasoline was in short supply, and for 444 days the humiliation of Iran's Ayatollah Khomeini holding 52 American hostages had dominated headlines and airwaves around the globe.

In a pre-campaign address from the oval office, Carter had blamed Americans for a "crisis of confidence." "For the first time in history," he said, "a majority of our people believe that the next five years will be worse than the past five years."

Carter's solution? "We must face the truth" of these dire national circumstances.[1]

How the Gipper Got Buy-In

In stark contrast, Ronald Reagan, the former broadcaster, actor, and governor of California, painted a picture, at every campaign appearance, of a national renewal, a "Morning in America." Voters bought into Reagan's *strategic story* in a huge way, handing him an electoral landslide.

Through his inaugural address, Reagan made certain that Congress, whose buy-in he would need next, heard his story loud and clear.

"It is time to reawaken this industrial giant," Reagan asserted, "to get government back within its means, and to lighten our punitive tax burden. And on these principles, there *will* be no compromise." With regard to international threats posed by Khomeini and our Cold War rival, the Soviet Union, the new President's strategic story went this way: "When action is required to preserve our national security, we *will* act. We *will* maintain sufficient strength to prevail."[2]

I've intentionally italicized the word *will* in Reagan's text to emphasize the trademark of all effective strategic stories: They project—without ifs, ands, or buts—that the future *will* be bright.

Reagan's "Morning in America" strategic storyline was so compelling that it proved difficult, even for his political enemies, *not* to buy into. From inauguration day forward, Reagan literally governed with this story, won re-election with it in 1984, and never departed from its fundamental structure, wherever he appeared.

Whatever your politics, it's hard to deny Reagan's extraordinary track record of generating buy-in for his legislative programs—from the Reagan tax revolution to the largest military buildup in American history—during his White House years.

In his farewell address on January 11, 1989, Reagan said: "I won a nickname: 'The Great Communicator.' But I never thought it was my style or the words I used that made a difference. It was the content. I wasn't a great communicator, but I communicated great things."[3]

Precisely. Reagan communicated one helluva of a strategic story.

Neutron Jack Brings Good Things to Life

The very same year that Ronald Reagan assumed office, the son of a railroad conductor from Massachusetts took the helm at the giant company for which Reagan had once been the television spokesman.

"Jack Welch's transformation at GE is an excellent example of a leader creating a story for the future,"[4] according to Noel Tichy, business professor at the University of Michigan.

John F. Welch, Jr. became CEO of a General Electric Corporation that was drowning in its own bureaucracy. An entrepreneur at heart, Welch foresaw the decades ahead as the most brutal in business history. He didn't believe that the predictable, lumbering GE could survive its competition, without being reborn in a very different form.

In order to "arouse the passions of GE's thousands of workers," says Tichy, Welch needed to "craft a story they could buy into."

Unlike Reagan, Welch was not a trained or polished speaker. In fact, traces of a childhood stutter remained with him well into his adult years. But Welch designed a strategic story that, like Reagan's "Morning in America," projected a clear image of a successful tomorrow.

If General Electric would embrace the massive layoffs and restructuring he advocated, Welch vowed it would become "The Winningest Company in the World," a solid "Number 1 or Number 2" in all of its businesses.

"Almost from the day he started as CEO, Welch began telling his story," according to Tichy. Through the many story-tellings and years ahead, *Welch made certain that his story of the future never changed, regardless of current circumstances.*

"Neutron Jack," as Welch became known for his passion and occasional ruthlessness, built his story of the future around three key messages, a time-tested methodology we'll examine closely later in this book.

Welch's story promised that General Electric's employees would experience a corporate future:

MESSAGE 1: "WHERE IDEAS WIN"
MESSAGE 2: "WHERE PEOPLE FLOURISH AND GROW"
MESSAGE 3: "WHERE THE EXCITEMENT OF THEIR WORK LIVES
           IS TRANSFERRED TO THEIR WHOLE LIVES."

You can fill an entire business library with volumes describing the initiatives and processes—from Six Sigma to globalization to e-business—that Welch put forward to make his strategic story a reality.

But in his own book, *Jack: Straight from the Gut*, Welch articulated what he saw as the driving force behind his achievements: "By 1985," Welch wrote, "the buy-in had begun."[5]

Over the twenty years that Welch was its chairman, CEO, and chief story-teller, GE's stock price climbed 2,876 percent. When he stepped down in the fall of 2001, the company he had built was, far and away, the most valuable company on earth.

And by the calculations of many tens of thousands of GE employees and shareholders, it was, indeed, the winningest.

The Greatest Buy-In Stories Ever Told

Welch and Reagan keenly appreciated what the most effective leaders—from business, to politics and government, to the military, to religion—have known through the ages.

"The key to leadership, as well as to the garnering of a following," Harvard's Howard Gardner wrote in his book, *Leading Minds,* "is effective communication of a story."[6]

Napoleon Bonaparte explained his own use of strategic stories this way: "*The human race is governed by its imagination.*" Thus, said Napoleon, knowing how to capture and manage that imagination means to exert tremendous influence and power.

History is replete with examples.

The stories of the great spiritual leaders—Moses, Jesus, Confucius, Mohammed, and Buddha—all promising a bright future, continue to mold the beliefs and behavior of billions of people today.

The United States of America was literally born of a strategic story that triggered a revolution. The "American Dream" of life, liberty, and the pursuit of happiness, as projected in the Declaration of Independence by its principal authors, Thomas Jefferson, John Adams, and Benjamin Franklin, remains unique in its power to inspire and motivate men and women everywhere.

Power for Good *and* Evil

But the record also shows that this language of buy-in can be applied in horribly toxic ways. In his seminal book, *Mein Kampf,* Adolf Hitler wrote of the importance of "finding an appropriate psychological form that will arrest the attention and appeal to the hearts" of a German people suffering from defeat in the first World War.[7]

The form that Hitler would discover and deploy in his stirring speeches and giant rallies—the Führer's story of future German dominance and ethnic supremacy—triggered enough buy-in to turn him into both one of the most idolized and most destructive figures of all time.

Fortunately, the strategic stories of Winston Churchill and Franklin Roosevelt were the prevailing influences in World War II.

Though accused by his domestic political foes of "starry-eyed" dreaming, FDR galvanized the American spirit through his famous fireside chats. Said Roosevelt, in his July 28, 1943 broadcast, "we *shall* not settle for less than total victory" against the Nazis and the Japanese.[8]

Seeking, from millions, the buy-in necessary to win the war in Europe, Churchill personified Hitler as "a monster of wickedness." He vowed, "we *shall* defend our island, whatever the cost may be . . . we *shall* fight on the beaches . . . we *shall* fight in the fields and in the streets." He promised the British people a victorious future if they *"never, never, never"* gave in.[9]

You know the rest of this story.

CHAPTER 3

How Strategic Stories Will Get You Twenty-First Century Buy-In

They who tell the stories rule the world.

—Native American medicine woman

We've seen that the language of strategic stories has stood the test of time, exerting its influence through the ages. But why is this language more relevant and powerful today than ever? And how will mastering it now provide you a unique competitive advantage in the workplace and marketplace?

The answer is *access and impact*. Strategic stories will provide you the key to the "lock-box" of twenty-first-century buy-in: people's attention, emotions, and memories.

You Will Capture People's Attention

More than five decades into the information age, we're suffering from Attention Deficit Disorder on a global scale.

Where once there was space, now there's cyberspace, crammed with two billion Web sites. Where there was quiet, there are cell phones, cordless phones, telemarketers, pagers, and the Airport Channel. We have voicemail, e-mail, junk mail, FedEx, faxes, newspapers, 24-hour news networks, newsletters, newsmagazines, and news groups.

On this brutal mental battlefield, "you have to earn the right for someone to pay attention," says Andrew Robertson, president of BBDO, the giant ad agency. "You need something with that magical ability to capture, hold and engage" people.[1]

Boundless advertising, marketing, and political research show that the magic key is a story. *Remember, stories are the language of our minds. We "think" in stories.* So, it follows that "stories offer fast access," according to Ken Sacharin, media director at Young and Rubicam. "They can get attention anytime, any place."[2]

Stories not only capture, they *expand*, our attention, and with it, our enjoyment of time. Why else would tens of millions of over-communicated, overstressed people willingly glue themselves to TV sitcoms, dramas, and "reality-based" stories, night after night, year after year?

And, while the set is on, the modern masters of influence are working their wizardry, packaging their products, services, and ideas within, you guessed it, strategic commercial stories.

These folks know something worth billions and billions of buy-in dollars.

> STRATEGIC STORIES ARE THE KEY TO CAPTURING
> TWENTY-FIRST CENTURY ATTENTION.

You Will Influence People's Emotions

Once strategic stories grab attention, they capitalize on it. To borrow a storyline from AT&T's writers, stories "reach out and touch someone," a connection which is crucial to generating true buy-in.

In today's data blizzard, blanketing people with *more* information—stats, graphs and charts, factoids—is not sufficient to win them over. The proverbial "data dump" has become counterproductive.

"We *know* we should eat less and exercise more. Right? Do we do it? No way,"[3] says Kevin Roberts, CEO Worldwide of Saatchi & Saatchi Advertising.

The route to real buy-in—to generating people's understanding, commitment and, ultimately, their action—is to impact, not just their thinking, but their emotions.

Which is precisely what stories do.

Watch the people around you in a darkened movie theater sometime. Though "it's only a story," they will laugh, cry, cringe, shake, and sigh. Then, they'll go out and purchase millions of dollars in movie-related merchandise!

"This is not a touchy-feely prescription," says leading neuroscientist Antonio Damasio. "Emotions are a very intelligent way to drive an organism toward certain outcomes."[4]

Strategic stories provide the capability to evoke, in a target audience, virtually any emotion or feeling. Here are some prime examples:

- In 1996, President Bill Clinton's campaign strategists created a storyline that characterized Clinton as *"a bridge to the twenty-first century."* It helped trigger enough confidence among voters to get him re-elected by a landslide, despite mounting evidence of personal improprieties.

- In its advertising, the Motel 6 chain evokes coziness, security, and a bright future in which *"We'll Leave the Light on For You"* if you head their way off the highway at night, which many thousands of travelers do.

- The U.S. Navy's strategic story tells potential recruits *"It's Not a Job, It's an Adventure,"* inspiring enough excitement, every year, to get thousands of volunteers to enlist.

In the twenty-first century, appealing to people's intellect may get you to first base, but it won't get you home. For that, you need to impact their emotions.

"The essential difference" says neurologist Donald Caine, "is that reason leads to conclusions, while emotion leads to action."[5]

STRATEGIC STORIES ARE THE KEY TO INFLUENCING TWENTY-FIRST-CENTURY EMOTIONS.

You Will Program People's Memories

The penultimate power of strategic stories is that their impact is never-ending. They effortlessly replay themselves, generating buy-in for days, years, even decades to come.

How many bible stories still influence your behavior? How many success stories have helped mold your attitudes? How many sports or love stories have guided your actions? How many business stories impact your decisions everyday?

"A story is like mental software" says researcher Annette Simmons. Thus, strategically designing a story "is as close as you can get to programming someone else's brain."[6]

"Within an Arm's Reach of Desire"

In the 1920s, Coca-Cola president Robert Woodruff created a strategic story for "internal consumption" by employees. His objective was to increase their commitment and productivity in order to grow Coke's market share.

Make sure that Coke is always "Within an Arm's Reach of Desire," and your future at the company will be bright. This was Woodruff's strategic storyline, according to Donald Keough, former president of Coca-Cola, who told me the background of the story and the fervent buy-in it triggered through the ranks.

"Every executive of the company created his or her future based on that story," said Keough. "That story created vending machines. You know, in my day, you used to travel by car. You'd go to a gas station and the first thing you'd do is pull open that box that had ice and cold Coca-Cola in it. That's how they put Coca-Cola within an arm's reach of desire. Then, the idea of fountain Coke in a cup or glass that you could get in restaurants or hotels was something that had to be created."

Over the years, Woodruff's strategic story, and the real-life stories it engendered, passed from employee to employee, nurturing an almost-evangelical corporate patriotism.

"A perfect example," said Keough, "is when the Berlin Wall came down. I remember coming into the office one day and people said, we've got to get in touch with our partners in West Germany to be sure that they can provide some free samples to these people who are busting through the wall from the Communist side.

"And I mean, with tears in their eyes, our German bottlers started to do that, putting cases of Coke in their cars, just to give these folks a little taste of freedom. It turned out to be one of the greatest marketing decisions in history, but, I promise you, it wasn't made that way."

Among Coca-Cola workers, the lasting power of Woodruff's story of Coke *Within An Arm's Reach of Desire,* Keough told me, "is a phenomenon so powerful you can't even understand it."[7]

Perhaps we can understand it.

We human beings "think" in stories. Once strategic stories grab our attention, they trigger our emotions and actions, then repeat themselves endlessly in our minds-eye, reinforcing their impact on our behavior, over and over again.

> **STRATEGIC STORIES ARE THE KEY TO PROGRAMMING TWENTY-FIRST-CENTURY MEMORIES.**

Whether you are a leader, manager, or marketer, your personal ability to develop and deliver your own strategic stories—which is what the rest of this book is about—will give you an extraordinary competitive edge in the years ahead.

Exhibit 3-1. Leading Brands, Leading Stories.

In 1886 a chemist named John Styth Pemberton concocted a drink of gooey brown syrup mixed with carbonated water and carried it, in jugs, to an Atlanta drugstore. This new soft drink, soon to be known as Coca-Cola, became quite popular in the years to follow. But in 1929, it emerged as a national phenomenon.

As America's economy crashed into the Great Depression, Coke's marketers transformed their product's image from a soda pop into a sunny story, a *"Pause That Refreshes"* in an otherwise gloomy world. It was a stroke of strategic brilliance that, even now, remains the fundamental storyline behind the number one brand on earth.

~~~~~~~~~~~~~~~~~~~

The McDonald's hamburger chain had about 700 stores in the mid-1960s, with sales of $171 million. By 1972, sales totaled more than $1 billion from the company's 2,200 outlets. What happened? A national TV advertising campaign that said virtually nothing about food.

Instead, it used music and images, reinforced by a clown named Ronald, to tell a strategic story of a positive future: McDonald's is *"Your Kind of Place . . . a Hap, Hap Happy Place"* where *"You Deserve A Break Today."*

Now the world's largest fast-food chain, McDonald's has more than 30,000 restaurants, with annual sales of nearly $4 billion. With ongoing refinements, such as "What You Want Is What You Get," the central storyline remains the same.

PART TWO

Speaking the Language of Buy-In

CHAPTER 4

A Framework for Buy-In

It should be bigger than you, so that other people can see themselves in this story you're painting.

> –Bill Stavropoulos
> Chairman & CEO
> Dow Chemical Company

What will it take to develop your own strategic stories? To personally "speak" this powerful language in your own buy-in challenges? Will the learning curve be steep and complicated? My experience with many thousands of executives, from generalists to technical experts, from managers to marketers to military officers, says no.

Why? Because in our personal lives, perhaps unwittingly, we develop *strategic stories* all the time. It's a natural way of relating to and getting buy-in from others.

If you've ever tried to influence a child, for instance, you've probably had an interaction similar to this:

Getting Buy-In

Adult: I'd really like you to clean up your room; it's a mess.
Child: Can't I do it later?

Adult: No, take a few minutes now.

Child: Just let me finish this game first.

Adult: No, now. It's better playing in a clean room.

Child: I can play fine the way it is.

Adult: A clean room means an orderly mind.

Child: (Mutters)

Adult: Enough! If you don't clean your room this minute, no television for a week.

Child: (Sobbing) I hate you! Nobody else has parents/relatives/teachers like you.

Adult: Okay, okay. Tell you what. If you clean your room now, we'll go out for a great lunch.

Child: Okay, but can we got to McDonald's?

Make it McDonald's and you can bet this youngster's room will be cleaned up in a matter of minutes. Why? Because the adult in this example has, if only out of desperation, designed a *story of a positive future* to which the child responds.

Don't get me wrong. I'm not advocating this as a child-rearing methodology. There are lessons, other than gratification, that young people need to learn.

But as a practical matter, as we've seen in the first part of this book, this is how buy-in works. People, big and little, are much more likely to do what *you* want if it leads to a future *they* want.

DEVELOPING A STRATEGIC STORY PROVIDES YOU A FRAME-WORK TO "CONNECT THE DOTS" BETWEEN THE FUTURE YOU WANT (YOUR OBJECTIVE) AND THE FUTURE YOUR AUDIENCE WANTS (THEIR AGENDA).

Chapters 5 to 9 of the book will show you how to design such a framework for generating buy-in from any target audience, in the workplace, marketplace, or public arena.

Exhibit 4-1 illustrates an invaluable tool: a step-by-step guide to the strategic story development process. Thereafter, to help you master it—to speak the language of buy-in—we'll examine each step through the real-life story of a CEO facing the biggest buy-in challenge of his career.

Exhibit 4-1. Strategic Story Methodology.

DEVELOPING YOUR STRATEGIC STORY

Goal Setting

DETERMINE YOUR BUY-IN OBJECTIVE

What action do you want your audience to take regarding your idea, proposal, product, service, or organization?

First Step

ESTABLISH YOUR STRATEGIC STORYLINE

To generate the action you want, what is the "big picture" or vision of a positive future you want your audience to see?

Second Step

DEVELOP YOUR STORYLINE IN THREE CHAPTERS THAT TARGET YOUR AUDIENCE'S AGENDA

What are *this* particular audience's needs, wants, and future goals?
In the future you are projecting, what are the three most important ways in which this audience's agenda will be fulfilled?

Third Step

CALL YOUR AUDIENCE TO ACTION

Ask for a commitment or first step toward the action you want.

CHAPTER 5

Developing Your Strategic Story

A leader or interest that can make itself master of current symbols is master of the current situation.

—Walter Lippman
Public Opinion (circa 1922)

Imagine owning, lock, stock, and formula, the number one product in your industry: a brand that has brought in billions of dollars, year after year, in sales. Then, one day, your competitors come along and, quite legally, take it away. Not only do they start manufacturing your product, they start selling it for a fraction of what you've been charging.

Think of General Motors building Toyota Camrys and marketing them for $5,000 a car, or Seven-Up brewing Coke and charging a nickel a bottle.

That's the kind of real-life nightmare the folks at one of the world's premier pharmaceutical companies were living as they gathered in New York for their annual sales meeting. Months earlier, their exclusive patent had expired on a blockbuster drug that had been one of the biggest sellers in medical history.

Now, hundreds of ace sales managers and representatives,

who had built their commissions and careers around this "golden pill" were gathered together, gossiping about calls from head-hunters and job offers from the competition. How could you blame them?

Already, their company was suffering a huge "generic erosion" of revenues, as other drug firms rushed in to market cheaper knock-off versions of what had been their leading product. And sales projections indicated that things would only get worse.

Entering the Buy-In Zone

"Thrown to the wolves" would be an understatement for most executives thrust into a situation like this. Yet this company's newly appointed CEO didn't view things that way.

Certainly, he appreciated the gravity of the moment. Simply put, if his sales staff left to sign on with the competition, he might as well turn out the lights behind them.

But this executive had faced tough audiences before. A former top sales rep himself, he saw this as another test, albeit the biggest yet, of the buy-in skills he had been honing throughout his career.

Stepping out into the spotlight, he began his remarks this way:

> I always wanted to be the Prozac product supervisor, with everyone nice and calm all around me. But they gave me Dramamine instead, to handle a rough ride. Folks, you gotta laugh!

And that they did, with eyebrows raised.

For here, before an audience of twelve hundred, was a rare bird, a "suit" from company headquarters who, apparently, was genuine enough to acknowledge the precariousness of his own situation. And confident enough to poke fun at it!

With his sense of irony and black humor, the CEO succeeded in connecting with his audience on a personal level.

Further, he set the stage, as intended, for the *strategic story* he had carefully developed to generate their buy-in that rainy day.

Let's examine how that story took shape.

Goal Setting

DETERMINE YOUR BUY-IN OBJECTIVE

Like any strategic process—from designing a building to planning a military campaign—developing a story for buy-in requires an initial exercise in goal setting, a beginning "with the end in mind." Thus, before outlining a single phrase of his presentation to his company's sales meeting, the pharmaceutical CEO tackled a pivotal question that all of us seeking buy-in must face:

What action do your want your audience to take?

Why should *action* be our goal in generating buy-in? Why not choose, as our objective, motivating a target audience to *think or feel* a certain way?

As we saw earlier in the book, impacting people's thoughts and emotions is, indeed, a crucial part of the buy-in equation. *But if we don't ultimately move them to act—to endorse our ideas, vote for us, approve our proposals, purchase our products or services—we have nothing to take to the bank.*

Simply put: *Action is buy-in's bottom line!*

In the case of the drug company CEO, generating understanding and good feelings would be indispensable. But it wouldn't be enough to save his job or organization.

The CEO's Objective: Retain and Motivate

The *action* the CEO needed was to have his sales force *stay*. And that wasn't all.

What if they stayed and sold at their current level of commitment and energy? Still insufficient. In order to survive and succeed in the new post-patent environment, he would need a sales force that produced faster and more effectively than the competition.

Thus, our CEO specified for himself a two-pronged objective: *to have his sales force stay and sell harder and smarter than ever,* despite the loss of his company's "golden pill."

With his buy-in objective clearly defined, he was positioned to build a strategic story that would take him where he wanted to go.

First Step

ESTABLISH YOUR STRATEGIC STORYLINE

"The beginning is the most important part of any work" wrote Plato, one of history's greatest storytellers, "for that is the time at which the character is formed and the desired impression more readily taken."[1]

Thus, the first step in developing—and later in delivering— your strategic story, is to establish its beginning and basic character. Writers call this the *storyline.*

The storyline is a strategic story's central message, title, and theme. Its purpose is to grab attention and communicate, in "big picture" terms, what the story's all about: a positive future!

How do you develop a strategic storyline? Brainstorming this question is a great way to start:

To generate the action you want,
What is the 'big picture' or vision of a positive future
You want your audience to see?

As we saw earlier, Ronald Reagan's campaign used the strategic storyline "Morning in America" to win voter approval in the 1980 presidential election. To generate support for the massive changes he initiated at General Electric, Jack Welch's storyline was "Winningest Company in the World."

Stepping onto the stage in New York, the drug-company CEO, who needed his target audience of salespeople to stay and work harder than ever, established his storyline this way:

> I wanted to visit with you personally this morning to share some feelings and thoughts I have about you, us, our company's future and what we will do to assure that future is what we all want it to be.

You, us, and a future we all want!

The moment the CEO delivered this storyline, the direction of the sales meeting began to change. Hundreds of sales managers and reps who had arrived with a very different story in their minds' eye—a future of gloom and doom—caught a glimpse of a new possibility. They began to imagine a future that might, conceivably, be bright.

Articulating a Positive Future

To deepen your understanding and further assist you in developing your own strategic storylines, or titles, Exhibit 5-1 lists a sampling of storylines deployed by leaders, companies, and organizations that, over the years, have been highly successful at generating buy-in.

Some storylines were created by individuals, others by marketing teams. A few were aimed at specific audiences. But most, like Reagan's "Morning in America," projected broad, generalized stories of a positive future that can be targeted at—and subsequently customized for—a variety of groups, stakeholders, and constituencies.

However the words flowed, all were designed to communicate the same basic compelling vision.

The future *will* be bright if you give us your buy-in!

Exhibit 5-1. Strategic Storylines.

AT&T
"Reach Out and Touch Someone"

Clinton for President
"Bridge to the 21st Century"

Coca-Cola
"The Pause that Refreshes"

Duke Energy
"We're Generating What's Next"

Federal Express
"Absolutely, Positively Overnight"

Fidelity Investments
"See Yourself Succeeding"

General Electric
"We Bring Good Things To Life"

G.W. Bush for President
"We Will Lead"

J.F. Kennedy
"The New Frontier"

Heineken
"Someday Soon the Best Will Come"

Home Depot
"Great Careers Built Here"

McDonald's
"You Deserve A Break Today"

Marlboro
"Come to Where the Flavor Is"

The Nature Conservancy
"We Preserve These Places Forever"

Microsoft
"Where Do You Want to Go Today?"

Motel Six
"We'll Leave the Lights on For You"

Reagan for President
"Morning in America"

U.S. Navy
"It's Not a Job, It's an Adventure"

Weyerhaeuser
"The Future Is Growing"

DEVELOP YOUR STORYLINE IN THREE CHAPTERS THAT TARGET YOUR AUDIENCE'S AGENDA

In January 2001, the U.S. Army violated its most sacred traditions, launching a multi-million dollar recruiting campaign that emphasized, of all things, personal individuality over uniformity and teamwork in the ranks.

The "Army of One" campaign that portrayed G.I. Joe and G.I. Jane as rugged, self-oriented individualists enraged old soldiers and veterans' groups. But it turned out to be a brilliant motivator, generating a level of buy-in far greater than imagined, within the Army's target audience of seventeen-to-twenty-four-year-olds.

State-of-the-art marketing research by Leo Burnett U.S.A, the Army's new ad agency, had shown that these Generation Yers were turned off by traditional images of duty, service, and sacrifice. Weaned on *Dawson's Creek* and *Buffy the Vampire Slayer*, they wanted to see themselves, even when part of a group, as unique and powerful individuals. Not the old "one for all," but rather, an "Army of One."

Risking large ad expenditures to heavily promote this new strategic storyline on such "new media" as the Internet and MTV, the army met its 2001 goal of 78,500 new recruits weeks ahead of schedule. This, following years of recruiting disappointments.

"A lot of people weren't sure that we crazy people were headed in the right direction," said Army Secretary Thomas E. White. "Well, I tell you, the proof's in the pudding."[2]

What the "Army of One" campaign underscored is this: What makes up a positive future depends on your audience's point-of-view.

What Is Your Audience's Agenda?

What kind of future do salespeople want? What about board members, colleagues, clients, customers, voters, or employees? Whether you're recruiting, leading, managing, politicking, or marketing, generating buy-in requires that you know *how your audience wants the future to be.*

What are this particular audience's needs, wants, and future goals?

This is the central question that underlies all twenty-first-century advertising, marketing, and political audience research. If we want people's buy-in, we need the answers, too.

Michael Quinlan, CEO of McDonald's Corporation for a decade, once summed it up for me this way: "Unless you can walk in their shoes, unless you're intelligent and sensitive enough to put yourself in their shoes," you won't get their buy-in. "You have to understand their hopes, their fears, their strengths, their weaknesses, their frustrations."[3]

"Then," according to Donald Keough, former president of Coca-Cola, "when you're ready to communicate with that group or that individual, you know what you're talking about."[4]

The CEO's Challenge: Targeting the Sales Force

Let's return to the case study of the pharmaceutical CEO. Standing before those twelve hundred salespeople, with the objective of retaining and motivating them, here was an executive who knew his target audience intimately.

Having *been* a sales rep early in his career, he had personally experienced the *needs, wants, and goals* of folks who work, largely, out of their automobiles, delivering drug samples and sales pitches to physicians and hospitals, from city to countryside. In the special parlance of drug reps, he had "carried the bag." Thus, he understood, first-hand, *what a positive future would look like from their point-of-view.*

- He knew that their most important need, having lost the patent on their "golden pill," was for new big-selling products.

- He recognized that they would want to be well compensated and supported during the lag time it takes for new products to become popular.

- He appreciated that, in addition to money, salespeople are motivated by personal factors such as recognition and pride.

Now, his challenge was to project his story of *"You, Us, and a Future We All Want"* in a way that would credibly fulfill *this* target audience's agenda.

Once again, he turned to what we all know, instinctively, about the way stories are structured: After the storyline or title, come the chapters!

His story would consist of three specially targeted chapters.

What Is a Targeted Chapter?

A *targeted chapter* is a projection of a future in which a target audience's specific needs, wants, and goals are fulfilled.

Each chapter begins with a *targeted message*, which asserts that an audience's agenda for the future *will* be fulfilled. It then goes on to provide credible *supporting evidence* that this assertion is true.

For example, Ronald Reagan's highly-successful 1980 "Morning in America" campaign story contained three targeted chapters, each built around a message that specifically targeted voter needs, wants, and goals, based on then-current polling research:

1. We *will* cut taxes and spur economic growth.

2. We *will* strengthen America's military.

3. We *will* reduce the size of government.

Reagan delivered his messages in campaign speeches, and then backed them up with evidential details of how, if elected, his tax, budget, and military plans would work. Together, his messages, plus the supporting evidence, made up the three chapters of the "Morning in America" strategic story that won him the White House.

Three Chapters of a Bright Tomorrow

Why did Ronald Reagan, Jack Welch, Winston Churchill, and so many other leaders seeking buy-in, all deliver strategic stories made up of three targeted chapters? Why, as we're about to see, did our pharmaceutical CEO do the same, at that crucial New York sales meeting?

The reason is an ancient formula, known as the "Rule of Three" or "Trilogy of Persuasion." A methodology used by masterful influencers, from prophets and attorneys to presidents and marketers, the Rule of Three is, structurally speaking, buy-in's Holy Grail. (In Chapter 6, we'll examine the Rule in detail.)

Exhibit 5-2 shows how the CEO's targeted chapters answer the key question: What are the three most important ways that the action *he* wants (having the sales force stay and sell harder than ever) will give the sales force the kind of bright tomorrow *they* want? The exhibit illustrates how his complete strategic story was structured to achieve his buy-in objective.

Out of respect for his privacy, I have rephrased his remarks, omitting or changing actual names and business data. I've also summarized the supporting evidence in his targeted chapters, for the sake of space and time. In reality, he took about forty minutes to deliver his presentation, which would decide the future of his company and career.

Exhibit 5-2. Pharmaceutical CEO's Strategic Story.

Buy-In Objective

Have Sales Force Stay and Work Harder

Strategic Storyline

You, Us, and a Future We All Want

I wanted to visit with you personally this morning to share some feelings and thoughts I have about you, us, our company's future, and what we will do to assure that future is what we all want it to be.

TARGETED CHAPTER 1

Targeted Message (Audience's Agenda: New Products)

This company, based on our pipeline of medicines and your time-tested performance as a sales force, is and will remain the best-positioned pharmaceutical firm in our industry.

Supporting Evidence

Starting later this year, we will bring to market, each and every year, a minimum of two important new drugs. I define that word "important" in actual dollar terms, words that you and I as salespeople can connect with. I know what's in our R&D pipeline and I can assure you, having reviewed it thoroughly, that we will deliver on that commitment.

(Summary: He describes, in detail, the types of new drugs under development, their status, and the market to which they will be targeted.)

TARGETED CHAPTER 2

Targeted Message (Audience's Agenda:
Compensation and Support)

We've undertaken a careful review of budgets everywhere in our company. What you need to know is that we will put more money, not less, into things that impact and improve your performance. We will increase our investment in you to make you even more successful.

Supporting Evidence

Where will we invest our dollars? In more sales training and development, more people, better sales support, and, as you are about to see, much better compensation for performance. We know this makes sense. Together, we will grow our way into the future.

(Summary: He continues by unveiling a new compensation package which, combined with investments in sales training and support, would enable the sales force to hit new sales targets and earn bigger commissions than ever, despite the loss of their leading product).

(Continued)

Exhibit 5-2. *(Continued)*

TARGETED CHAPTER 3

Targeted Message (Audience's Agenda: Recognition and Pride)

We will always appreciate you. I am here today to tell you that there's a clear understanding on the part of senior management that it is you and your performance that have fueled the success of this company.

Supporting Evidence

This could not have been made clearer to me than it was last week. I was at a conference in Los Angeles. An old friend introduced me to a hospital administrator I'd never met. And right away that woman said to me, "I want to tell you that I think your firm is extraordinary. Why? Because of your salesperson. The level of service she provides our hospital goes way beyond the call of duty. And it has given me a feel for the kind of people and the kind of company you are."

What she said brought home to me what I have always known. That you are what makes our company great. And, in this case, I want to say a special thanks to Mary Richardson (gesturing) . . . I'm so very proud of her and of each and every one of you.

Note: Mary Richardson was promoted from Sales Representative to District Manager shortly thereafter.

Third Step

CALL YOUR AUDIENCE TO ACTION

Shakespeare said, "by your entrances and exits shall ye be known."[5] So it is with every strategic story and storyteller seeking buy-in.

Entering that New York sales meeting, our pharmaceutical CEO had taken a calculated risk. He had let the men and women he employed know his vulnerabilities and the uphill struggle he and the company faced.

Despite that challenge, he had told a strategic story that projected a positive future in which their specific agenda—needs, wants, and goals—could be fulfilled.

Now was the moment he had worked toward.

With the end of a strategic story comes the opportunity to make your objective clear. Now is the time to ask your audience to take the actions you're proposing, to call on them to "come along" and make the story come true.

Now is when the buy-in gets real.

For this CEO to succeed, despite the loss of his leading product, he would need his sales force to stay and market new products at ever-increasing levels of energy and commitment.

Exhibit 5-3 shows his Call-to-Action.

Exhibit 5-3. Call-to-Action.

Let's prove to our industry, to our customers, to ourselves, how truly unstoppable this sales force is. Let's show them that there is not a single target or goal that, together, we cannot attain. Let's build that future we all want. And I have no doubt that we can, because we'll provide you everything you need to succeed. Do I have your commitment going forward?

So, What Was the Outcome?

The CEO, indeed, won their commitment and achieved his buy-in objective in a big way. Not only did he retain the sales force, including the top performers, he expanded it significantly in the years following his New York presentation.

Despite the loss of a hugely successful product, his company maintained strong sales and brought numerous new big-selling drugs to the marketplace.

He retired as one the most accomplished leaders in his field, revered by former colleagues and employees for his tireless dedication to their wants and needs, and respected industry-wide for his exemplary skills at generating buy-in.

CHAPTER 6

The Rule of Three

When people ask me about this company I tell them three things.

—Steve Ballmer
CEO
Microsoft

Earth, Wind, Fire

Animal, Vegetable, Mineral

Life, Liberty, Pursuit of Happiness

Easy as 1-2-3

The fact that the universally known phrases above share a common arithmetic is no coincidence. There's a strategic calculus behind them that has played a leading role in shaping man's thinking for as long as history can recall. It has come to be known, as noted in the last chapter, as the "Rule of Three."

The Rule of Three:

THE MIND MOST EASILY RECEIVES, RETAINS, AND RECALLS INFORMATION PRESENTED TO IT IN THREES.

No one really knows how or why the Rule came to be. Were we born with some subconscious 1,2,3 in our DNA? Or was it later plugged, by someone or something, into our mental circuitry? Like the conundrum of the chicken and the egg, it's a riddle without an answer.

What can be established is that the practice of leveraging the Rule—of communicating in threes to enhance audience reception, retention, and recall—dates, at least, to the Greek mythologists of the eighth century B.C.

According to the famous myth of the Three Fates, man's destiny is ruled by: (1) Clothos, who spins out the threads of life, (2) Lachesis, who draws out each thread to determine one's life story, and (3) Atropos, who cuts the threads to signify death. Good fortune will come from acknowledging and working with each of the fates, or so the legend goes.

Whatever the case, from that point forward, our collective consciousness has been saturated with threes.

Father, Son, Holy Ghost

Faith, Hope, Charity

Our Lives, Our Fortune, Our Sacred Honor

Body, Mind, Spirit

Duty, Honor, Country

Past, Present, Future

Red, White, and Blue

Ready, Aim, Fire

On Your Mark, Get Set, Go

See No Evil, Hear No Evil, Speak No Evil

Lights, Camera, Action

Reading, 'Riting, 'Rithmetic

Sex, Drugs, Rock 'n Roll

3-Ring Circus

You Get Three Wishes

Three Strikes and You're In

Fast forward to the twenty-first century.

How do *you* feel when someone makes a speech with fourteen key points you're supposed to remember? Tries to sell you on eleven things about their product? Wants you follow a ten-step process?

It's a wonder they continue to try.

Audience research shows that most folks begin to lock their mental gates at the very thought of having to listen to, let alone remember, another litany of factoids.

But, three ideas! Three steps! Three reasons! For this, the mind's portal opens. We feel an immediate sense of relief. And, if we're interested in the topic, it becomes easy, even enjoyable to focus.

That's the ancient Rule of Three at work in today's overstressed, overcommunicated environment. And it's an axiom that many of the most savvy leaders, marketers, and organizations have taken to heart.

Here are (guess how many) examples:

- Chinese President Jiang Zemin redefined Marxism and, over a thirteen-year period, transformed his nation's economy into a semi-entrepreneurial state, by ceaselessly promoting his famous "theory of the three represents." The theory stated that the modern communist party should represent:

1. The most advanced forces of production

2. The most advanced forces of culture

3. The fundamental interests of the broadest number of people

■ The Ritz-Carlton hotel chain trains its employees to always take "three steps of service" when interacting with guests. As specifically written into the hotel's credo, the steps are:

1. A warm and sincere greeting.

2. Anticipation and compliance with guest needs.

3. A fond farewell. Give guests a warm good-bye and use their names if and when possible.

■ After becoming chairman and CEO of the Ford Motor Company, which his great-grandfather founded, William Clay Ford, Jr. announced that his company's strategy for the twenty-first century was to "build a stronger business" by making its automobiles more affordable in three ways:

1. Economically

2. Environmentally

3. Socially ("a great way," said Ford, "to honor our past and secure our future")[1]

The Power of Three in Buy-In

How, then, does the wisdom of threes apply to the specific challenge we're focused on in this book—the challenge of communicating, not only for understanding and recall, but for a target audience's support, commitment, and action? How does it map on to the language of buy-in?

Directly. If people welcome information delivered in threes, it stands to reason that they'll react the same way to strategic stories designed with this formula in mind.

Thus, the common structure of the buy-in stories we've examined thus far—Ronald Reagan's, Jack Welch's, and the pharmaceutical CEO's—and those we'll see in the pages ahead, makes eminent sense.

Strategic Story of a Positive Future

STRATEGIC STORYLINE. *THREE TARGETED CHAPTERS WITH SUPPORTING EVIDENCE.* CALL-TO-ACTION.

With our deepened appreciation for the power of three, let's continue our journey into the language of strategic stories. In the next chapter, we'll look at its application in times of controversy and crisis, when buy-in is critically important and especially hard to get.

CHAPTER 7

When Times Get Tough, the Smart Get Buy-In

I could a tale unfold whose lightest word would harrow up thy soul.

Shakespeare, *Hamlet*, Act I

Inside Intel

In mid-1994, a flaw was discovered in millions of Pentium chips, the newest technology from Intel, the largest manufacturer of personal computer "brains" in the world.

As word spread on the Internet, worried customers contacted Intel headquarters in Santa Clara, California. On instructions from CEO Andy Grove, they were told that no technology was perfect, that the glitch only affected high-level scientific computations, and that, for the average computer user, a problem might crop up "once in 27,000 years."[1]

For PC owners, that wasn't good enough.

They placed calls to CNN, *The New York Times*, and *The Wall Street Journal*. Next came media coverage that prompted IBM to publicly halt all shipments of Pentium-based PCs. That, in turn, triggered a stock slide that cost Intel more than a billion dollars in market value in a matter of just a few days.

Said *Time* magazine, the turn of events was the "biggest iceberg" ever hit by CEO Grove and his "hyper-rational" team of engineers.[2]

But within the titanic crisis they faced was an extraordinarily valuable lesson:

The best way out of bad news, crisis, and controversy, is to generate buy-in for a positive future, rather than dwell on the problems of the past.

Scientifically brilliant though he was, what Andy Grove had missed was this: Customers didn't want excuses or a technical analysis of the Pentium chip. They wanted to know that their computing needs, wants, and goals for the future would, unequivocally, be met.

When that realization finally sank in, Grove moved forward, with the help of communication experts, to develop a strategic story for the purpose of regenerating customer commitment.

Its targeted messages were carefully engineered to address this key question (first noted in Chapter 5), which is rooted in the Rule of Three:

IN THE FUTURE YOU ARE PROJECTING, WHAT ARE THE THREE MOST IMPORTANT WAYS IN WHICH THIS AUDIENCE'S AGENDA WILL BE FULFILLED?

From the many angry calls received, Intel had more than sufficient research on what its target audience needed and wanted: the option of receiving replacement Pentium chips at no cost or inconvenience, and assurances that any future problems would be quickly and reliably handled.

Exhibit 7-1 lists the key elements of the strategic story Intel ultimately communicated—via the media, corporate announcements, and a telephone hot line—to win back customer buy-in. Once again, the supporting evidence in each targeted chapter has been summarized.

Exhibit 7-1. Intel's Strategic Story.

Buy-In Objective

Keep Customers Buying Intel Products

Strategic Storyline

Intel Will Always Put Customers First

TARGETED CHAPTER 1

Targeted Message (Audience's Agenda: Replacement Chips)

Intel will provide free replacement Pentium chips to anyone who wants them.

Supporting Evidence

(Summary: Details of the recall and replacement program are explained.)

TARGETED CHAPTER 2

Targeted Message (Audience's Agenda: Convenience)

Intel will provide in-home or office service to those who want chips replaced.

Supporting Evidence

(Summary: Details of the in-home or office service are explained.)

TARGETED CHAPTER 3

Targeted Message (Audience's Agenda: Reliability)

Intel will always stand behind everything it makes and, should anything go wrong with its products, will move quickly to make things right.

Supporting Evidence

(Summary: New Intel corporate policy regarding recalls is explained).

CALL-TO-ACTION

Continue to trust Intel and purchase computers with the "Intel Inside" logo.

How many computer owners, do you think, actually asked for replacement chips? Hardly any. The vast majority of PC users never had any intention of doing the kind of sophisticated mathematics that could potentially trigger the Pentium's tiny flaw.

It was the company's initial response, not its technology, that had turned customers sour on Intel.

Outcome

Once the correct decision was made, and the right strategic story was communicated, Intel regained its market value and reputation. In fact, it ultimately benefited from the attendant publicity, as consumers began to admire the company's commitment to making things right.

The experience was, CEO Grove later said, "a difficult education."[3]

To say the least. And it is one that need not be suffered by you or others. Just keep this in mind:

WHEN THE GOING GETS ESPECIALLY TOUGH, THE SMARTEST EXECUTIVES GENERATE BUY-IN.

Here are two more examples of executives who, in extremely trying circumstances, did just that.

WorldCom Comes Clean

In April 2002, John Sidgmore became interim CEO of deeply-troubled long distance giant WorldCom. In the wake of the telecommunications implosion of 2000 to 2001 and the resignation of company founder Bernard Ebbers, WorldCom was reported to be some $30 billion in debt.

On the day he took the CEO job, Sidgmore said that he could not have imagined that things would yet become billions of dollars worse.[4] But just two months later, WorldCom was forced to fire its chief financial officer and disclose a string of improperly stated earnings that dated back at least three years.

Sidgmore, who testified that "the misdeeds occurred before I became CEO," found himself with the task of eliminating more than 17,000 jobs and, in the throws of a very public bankruptcy, rehabilitating the WorldCom that was left.

To be successful, he badly needed buy-in from five key audiences: present and future employees, federal regulators, shareholders, creditors, and key customers, including the Department of Defense.

With those targets in mind, he articulated his strategic story at the National Press Club in Washington, D.C., excerpts of which are presented in Exhibit 7-2.

Exhibit 7-2. Excerpts from WorldCom CEO's Press Conference at the National Press Club, July 2, 2002.

Buy-In Objective

Have Key Stakeholders
Continue Working with WorldCom

Strategic Storyline

We Can Work Together to Build the Future

WorldCom is a very key component of our nation's economy and communications infrastructure. Even after our recent layoffs we still have over sixty-thousand employees and millions of investors. I really feel confident that we can work together to build the future.

TARGETED CHAPTER 1

Targeted Message (Audience's Agenda: Transparency & Action)

We will be straight about our problems. I can promise you that. And we will take the necessary steps to aggressively solve them. We will work very hard to regain your trust.

Supporting Evidence

(Summary: Details of new accounting and auditing procedures.)

(Continued)

Exhibit 7.2. *(Continued)*

TARGETED CHAPTER 2

Targeted Message (Audience's Agenda: Customer Service)

We are committed to providing great service to our customers not just to-day but also tomorrow.

Supporting Evidence

(Summary: Details of new initiatives to retain customers with improved products and service.)

TARGETED CHAPTER 3

Targeted Message (Audience's Agenda: New Business Plan)

We will return your faith in us with renewed value and the best telecommunications company anywhere in the world.

Supporting Evidence

(Summary: Details of efforts to strengthen executive team and develop new business plan.)

CALL-TO-ACTION

Today, we're here to tell you that WorldCom needs the help and understanding and patience of our customers, of our suppliers, of our lenders, and of the American people.

Outcome

Although the level of concern in target audiences remained high, Sidgmore was generally credited with bringing a new level of transparency to WorldCom operations, positioning it to successfully restructure during bankruptcy and bringing in a new senior executive team.

Anthrax Attacks

Five weeks after the September 11, 2001 attacks on the World Trade Center and Pentagon, an anthrax-filled letter bomb, addressed to U.S. Senate Majority Leader Tom Daschle, was delivered to Room 509 in the Hart Senate Office Building.

When the envelope was opened and white powder seeped out, Daschle wasn't present. But the thirty-one staffers who were tested positive for anthrax exposure within a matter of days.

Similar anthrax letters had been sent to TV network offices in New York and to the *National Enquirer* in Florida, where one infected employee was close to death and later died.

The new anthrax scare hit hard in the corridors of the U.S. Capitol. How many more letters had been delivered? And where?

Word passed that the House of Representatives was about to shut down. But on the Senate side, Tom Daschle was adamant. To cut and run, he believed, would send a signal to terrorists around the world, that the government of the United States, home of the brave, was very afraid.

A veteran of innumerable political campaigns, Daschle recognized the challenge before him: Assess the needs of his Senate colleagues and employees, then deliver a strategic story that would generate enough buy-in to keep calm their fears and keep them at work.

Excerpts of Daschle's story, delivered before TV cameras, with anthrax and medical experts at his side, are shown in Exhibit 7-3.

Exhibit 7-3. Excerpts from U.S. Senator Tom Daschle's Statement at the U.S. Capitol, October 16, 2001.

Buy-In Objective

Have U.S. Senate and Staff Remain Calm Despite Anthrax Letters

Strategic Storyline

Everyone Will Be Okay

I just want to report that thirty-one people have now had positive nasal swabs. There's a huge difference between a positive nasal swab, which only indicates anthrax exposure, of course, and infection. There is absolutely no evidence of infection at this point. All of those who have had this positive nasal swab have been on antibiotics, now, for some time.

The good news is that everyone will be okay. I am very confident about that, given the medication and the fact that it was provided early and is continuing to be provided. I'm concerned for my staff, I'm angered that this has happened. But I feel very confident about the fact that everyone will be okay. And I feel extremely good about the process we have employed all the way through to this time. I want to talk just briefly about three things.

(Continued)

Exhibit 7.3. *(Continued)*

TARGETED CHAPTER 1

Targeted Message (Audience's Agenda:
Leadership and Assurance)

First of all, it is my strong determination and Senator (Trent) Lott's, as well, that we will not let this stop the work of the Senate.

Supporting Evidence

There will be a vote this afternoon, we will be in session and have a vote or votes tomorrow, and I am absolutely determined to assure that the Senate continues to do its work.

TARGETED CHAPTER 2

Targeted Message (Audience's Agenda: Information)

Secondly, I want to accommodate those who are understandably interested in acquiring as much information as possible about the environment in our Senate office buildings.

Supporting Evidence

We will accommodate their needs and provide extra precautionary efforts to assure that they can go in and check the progress on additional environmental questions that we hope to resolve in the not-too-distant future.

TARGETED CHAPTER 3

Targeted Message (Audience's Agenda: Medical Attention)

And finally, I think it's important to emphasize that we are going to work in concert with all of the medical personnel. We have the single best medical personnel in the world to address this.

Supporting Evidence

They've already come on site. We've been working very closely with the Department of Health and Human Services. And Scott Lillibridge from HHS will be here in just a moment to talk about their efforts. We have extraordinary people doing all that they can to ensure that we can bring this matter to a successful conclusion.

CALL-TO-ACTION

Circumstances are well in hand. Now, let me take your questions.

Outcome

The Republican-controlled House of Representatives, to the alarm of many Americans, closed down for five days. But on the other side of the Capitol, the Senate, led by Democrat Tom Daschle, stayed at work, with the blessing of GOP leader Trent Lott, who said: "We think we've made the right decision to stay in session here and have votes today and probably tomorrow. I feel confident we can get our work done while taking necessary precautions to protect the people that work with us."

Conclusion

To underscore the key insights of this chapter:

THE BEST WAY OUT OF BAD NEWS, CRISIS, AND CONTROVERSY IS TO GENERATE BUY-IN FOR A POSITIVE FUTURE, RATHER THAN DWELL ON THE PROBLEMS OF THE PAST. WHEN THE GOING GETS ESPECIALLY TOUGH, THE SMARTEST EXECUTIVES GENERATE BUY-IN.

CHAPTER 8

The Charisma Quotient

Leadership is one of the performing arts and the leader always has to sell himself or herself to the audience.

—Warren Bennis
Leadership author and educator

When I left CNN to begin working with corporate and government leaders, I was struck by what so many had been led to believe was the key to generating buy-in.

Executives wanted to know if, after fifteen years of on-camera network television experience, I could train them to *appear more charismatic* and, thus, be more effective at influencing others.

I gave them something far more powerful.

I taught them the exact same methodology—the language of buy-in—I've been sharing with you in this book. Not because it's some fancy theory, but because I had seen it work in the real world, time and time again.

From the numerous examples we've looked at together, you've now seen it, too. The strategic story methodology is simply unparalleled in molding the thoughts and emotions of a target audience, in bad times or good.

But there's a remarkable icing on this cake: A well-designed strategic story can literally reshape the storyteller, too!

Bush's New Gravitas

On September 20, 2001, nine days after Al Qaeda terrorists crashed commercial airliners into the World Trade Center and Pentagon, President George W. Bush, heretofore a notably uncharismatic officeholder, stepped to the rostrum of the U.S. House of Representatives.

During his razor-margin campaign against Al Gore and subsequent seven months in the Oval Office, the rap against Bush—from both friend and political foe—was that he couldn't ad-lib without evoking strange "Bushisms" and, when scripted, came across as disjointed, even bumbling. Some called Bush "oratorically challenged."

But that evening, before a global television audience of eighty-two million, George W. Bush was visibly transformed. His pacing was perfect, his demeanor purposeful, his gestures unmistakably presidential. And not because he had been *trained* to appear that way.

Over the years, as a political candidate, governor, and incumbent President, Bush had participated in endless hours of public speaking training. None of it had worked.

What happened *this* night? Bush's ability to perform—his charisma quotient—rose to meet the substance of the words before him.

Bush arrived with a clear objective in mind, as he put it, a "mission:" to generate buy-in for an extended U.S. involvement overseas, a gradual recovery at home, and his ability to lead both.

And, at a very sad and frightening time in U.S. history, he came with a story of a positive future, a story that targeted his audience's needs, followed the age-old structural rules, and transformed the man who delivered it. Excerpts of the address appear in Exhibit 8-1.

Exhibit 8-1. Excerpts from President George W. Bush's Address to a Joint Session of Congress, September 20, 2001.

Buy-In Objective

Rally the Nation
In the Wake of September 11th Attacks
(War on Terrorism)

Strategic Storyline

An Age of Liberty

On September 11th, enemies of freedom committed an act of war against our country. Americans have known the casualties of war—but not at the center of a great city on a peaceful morning. Americans have known surprise attacks—but never before on thousands of civilians. Some speak of an age of terror. I know there are struggles ahead and dangers to face. But this country will define our times, not be defined by them. As long as the United States of America is determined and strong, this will not be an age of terror. This will be an age of liberty, here and across the world.

TARGETED CHAPTER 1

Targeted Message (Audience's Agenda: Justice)

Whether we bring our enemies to justice, or bring justice to our enemies, justice will be done.

Supporting Evidence

We will direct every resource at our command—every means of diplomacy, every tool of intelligence, every instrument of law enforcement, every financial influence, and every necessary weapon of war—to the disruption and to the defeat of the global terror network. We will starve terrorists of funding, turn them one against another, drive them from place to place, until there is no refuge or rest. And we will pursue nations that provide aid or safe haven to terrorism.

(Continued)

Exhibit 8-1. *(Continued)*

TARGETED CHAPTER 2

Targeted Message (Audience's Agenda: Security at Home)

We will take defensive measures against terrorism to protect Americans.

Supporting Evidence

Tonight I announce the creation of a Cabinet-level position reporting directly to me—the Office of Homeland Security. And tonight I also announce a distinguished American to lead this effort, to strengthen American security: a military veteran, an effective governor, a true patriot, a trusted friend—Pennsylvania's Tom Ridge. He will lead, oversee, and coordinate a comprehensive national strategy to safeguard our country against terrorism, and respond to any attack that may come.

TARGETED CHAPTER 3

Targeted Message (Audience's Agenda: Economic Recovery)

We will come together to take active steps that strengthen America's economy and put our people back to work.

Supporting Evidence

Terrorism attacked a symbol of American prosperity. They did not touch its source. America is successful because of hard work and creativity and the enterprise of our people. These were the true strengths of our economy before September 11th, and they are our strengths today. Tonight we welcome (gesturing) two leaders who embody the extraordinary spirit of New Yorkers: Governor George Pataki and Mayor Rudolph Guiliani. As a symbol of America's resolve, my administration will work with Congress and these two leaders to show the world that we will rebuild New York City.

CALL-TO-ACTION

Americans are asking: What is expected of us? I ask you to be calm and resolute, even in the face of a continuing threat. I ask you to uphold the values of America, and remember why so many have come here. I ask you to continue to support the victims of this tragedy with your contributions. I ask your continued participation and confidence in the American economy.

We will not tire, we will not falter, and we will not fail.

Buy-In Rating: 90 Percent

Following his forty-one minute address, Bush's job approval score—his buy-in rating among Americans—"jumped to 90 percent, the highest ever," for any president, according to the Gallup organization.[1] What's more, the jump represented "the largest rally effect" in presidential polling history.

Many, from average citizens to political pundits, were astounded by Bush's showing.

One presidential historian put it this way: "That night . . . Bush emerged as a leader who was thoroughly in command. Not once did he fumble a line or mangle a phrase. No longer did commentators say, after that performance, that Bush lacked gravitas, or did cartoonists depict him as a little boy miscast in a man's job. One showed him, hands firmly gripping the lectern, speaking out confidently while in the background FDR and Churchill applaud."[2]

Dramatic though it was, the source of the forty-third President's metamorphosis was no mystery to those in the know. For that night, George W. Bush spoke the language that so many of history's most charismatic leaders, including FDR, Churchill, and Ronald Reagan, have spoken. And, in the process, he discovered the special secret they so well understood.

COMMUNICATING A POSITIVE FUTURE IMPACTS NOT ONLY THE AUDIENCE BUT THE COMMUNICATOR, TOO.

In the way that a winning game plan inspires an athlete to excel, a great script moves an actor to perfection, or superb music brings out a tenor's brilliance, a strategic story of a positive future empowers the person who delivers it.

It boosts commitment. It maximizes focus and energy. Without artificially orchestrated body language, eye contact, or tone of voice, communicating a positive future generates natural charisma and with it, buy-in from one's audience.

General Colin Powell, Bush's Secretary of State, summed it up this way: "Optimism is a force multiplier."

Three Great Goals for America

The wellspring of power Bush tapped into on September 20th was not soon forgotten at his White House.

Three weeks later, Bush forcefully underscored the themes of his new strategic story during a formal prime-time news conference.

The New York Times, in its lead editorial the following day, wrote that Bush continued to communicate like "a different man than the one who was just barely elected. He seemed confident . . . sure of his purpose and in full command . . . in the wake of the terrible terrorist attacks of September 11. Mr. Bush should return to this and similar venues to talk to the American people."[3]

And that he would. In his subsequent State of the Union address, on January 29, 2002, Bush positioned his strategic story as not only the centerpiece of his speech, but as the central vision and future promise of his presidency.

To accelerate congressional and domestic political buy-in for his new budget proposals and priorities, his strategic storyline, or big picture of a positive future, was reframed, from "Age of Liberty" to "Three Great Goals for America."

Under this forward-looking banner headline, which canonized the Rule of Three, George W. Bush delivered a strategic story that reemphasized his primary targeted messages and provided newsworthy supporting evidence. Excerpts of the address appear in Exhibit 8-2.

Exhibit 8-2. Excerpts from President George W. Bush's State of the Union Address, January 29, 2002.

Buy-In Objective

Have Congress and the Public Support
Bush Administration Policies and Budget

Strategic Storyline

Three Great Goals for America

As we gather tonight, our nation is at war, our economy is in recession, and the civilized world faces unprecedented dangers. Yet the state of our union has never been stronger. My budget supports three great goals for America.

TARGETED CHAPTER 1

Targeted Message (Audience's Agenda: Justice and Victory)
We will win this war.

Supporting Evidence

We last met in an hour of shock and suffering. In four short months, our nation has comforted the victims, begun to rebuild New York and the Pentagon, rallied a great coalition, captured, arrested, and rid the world of thousands of terrorists, destroyed Afghanistan's terrorist training camps, saved a people from starvation, and freed a country from brutal oppression.

America and Afghanistan are now allies against terror. We will be partners in rebuilding that country, and this evening we welcome [gesturing] the distinguished interim leader of a liberated Afghanistan: Chairman Hamid Karzai.

The last time we met in this chamber, the mothers and daughters of Afghanistan were captives in their homes, forbidden from working or going to school. Today, women are free, and are part of Afghanistan's new government. And we welcome [gesturing] the new minister of women's affairs, Doctor Sima Samar.

It costs a lot to fight this war. We have spent more than a billion dollars a month, over $30 million a day, and we must be prepared for future operations.

(Continued)

Exhibit 8-2. *(Continued)*

TARGETED CHAPTER 2

Targeted Message (Audience's Agenda: Security at Home)

We will protect our homeland.

Supporting Evidence

My budget nearly doubles funding for a sustained strategy of homeland security focused on four key areas: bioterrorism, emergency response, airport and border security, and improved intelligence. We will develop vaccines to fight anthrax and other deadly diseases. We will increase funding to help states and communities train and equip our heroic police and firefighters. We will improve intelligence collection and sharing, expand patrols at our borders, strengthen the security of air travel, and use technology to track the arrivals and departures of visitors to the United States. Homeland security will make America not only stronger, but in many ways better.

TARGETED CHAPTER 3

Targeted Message (Audience's Agenda: Economic Recovery)

We will revive our economy.

Supporting Evidence

Once we have funded our national security and homeland security, the final great priority of my budget is economic security for the American people. When America works, America prospers, so my economic security plan can be summed up in one word: jobs. Good jobs begin with good schools, and here we've made a fine start. Good jobs depend on reliable and affordable energy. Good jobs depend on free trade. Good jobs depend on sound tax policy.

CALL-TO-ACTION

Members [of Congress] . . . I ask you to join me on these important domestic issues in the same spirit of cooperation we have applied to our war against terrorism. For too long our culture has said: If it feels good, do it. Now American is embracing a new ethic and a new creed: Let's roll.

Outcome

Through his 2002 State of the Union address, delivered with "plain-spoken eloquence . . . force and polish,"[4] according to reviewers, Bush completed his very public transformation from a likeable but lackluster politician, into a purposeful chief executive with the vision, communication skills, and charisma necessary to rally and lead his nation in peace or wartime.

In the months ahead, his "Three Great Goals for America," including a global war on terrorism, became the hallmark of his presidency and America's national agenda.

COMMUNICATING A STRATEGIC STORY OF A POSITIVE FUTURE WILL NOT ONLY IMPACT YOUR AUDIENCE, IT WILL EMPOWER YOU AS THE COMMUNICATOR, TOO!

CHAPTER 9

The Best Evidence

Connect with people's gut concerns and they'll go anywhere with you, without asking for details. Don't connect, and you'll never be able to show them enough details to get them to follow.

> –Thomas L. Friedman
> Columnist
> *The New York Times*

A salt-and-pepper bearded man with a striped robe over his sport coat. A diminutive female physician wearing pearl earrings and a scarf. A note from a seven-year-old boy. A Peruvian-born airline attendant with her arm in a sling.

All were present in the chamber of the U.S. House of Representatives as President Bush delivered the State of the Union address we examined in Chapter 8.

Interesting, but superfluous? Categorically not.

Each was strategically positioned in Bush's script and in the room that night, a meticulously timed trump card based on a powerful insight:

THE BEST SUPPORTING EVIDENCE FOR A STORY OR MESSAGE ABOUT THE FUTURE IS A CREDIBLE, REAL-LIFE EXAMPLE FROM YESTERDAY OR TODAY.

Nobel Prize winning psychologist Daniel Kahneman demonstrated this scientifically in the mid-1970s. In studies that challenged long-held views about decision making and provided the pillars of a brand new field, soon to be called behavioral economics, Kahneman and fellow researcher Amos Tversky established unequivocally that:

1. First impressions shape subsequent decisions.

2. Vivid examples are overwhelming more influential in shaping decisions than abstract information, even if the information is more accurate.

Simply stated, in formulating opinions and making choices, we're all in a rush to judgment and we hail from the show-me state. Further, it's not bullet points, numbers, slides, processes, or schematics we're looking for. We want to see the genuine item.

As Oscar-winner Cuba Gooding, Jr. shrieked repeatedly to Tom Cruise, who played his agent in the movie *Jerry McGuire,* skip the details and "show me the money!"

We all want the *real* thing.

The Real McCoy

Using real-life examples to shape opinions is a powerhouse approach that can be applied to any buy-in challenge.

Advertisers do it all the time. They fill their commercials with customers and celebrities who have personally tried their products. Lawyers seek out witnesses from the scene of the crime. Reporters look for people directly involved in a story. So do public relations practitioners and communication strategists.

Here's a behind-the-scenes example from my own experience.

A number of years back I was retained to advise the CEO of a major hospital association that was facing a political crisis in one of the fastest-growing western states.

Seeking quick budget reductions, the newly elected conservative governor had put state Medicaid payments on his "must cut" list for the new fiscal year. In the news media, he attacked the hospitals, and their association, as "fat cats" who were getting rich on government handouts.

The hospitals were terrified. It wasn't true. For years, Medicaid payments had constituted a critical percentage of rudimentary hospital income. Based on their calculations, most of the state's rural hospitals would be forced to shut their doors if the cuts became reality.

The governor and his big city legislative allies didn't seem to care.

On my second night in the state's capital, I flicked on the TV in my hotel room. Absent-mindedly changing channels, I hit on an episode of a reality-based show, *Rescue 911*, based on a dramatic incident that had occurred recently in that very state.

It was the story of Alex Bayless, an 18-year-old high school honor student and football star, who had been paralyzed in an accident on a river near his rural hometown. If not for the neurosurgeon at the small regional hospital, Alex would not have lived.

I knew immediately that I had happened on the *real thing*, the real-life evidence I needed to try to help save the state's rural hospitals from the governor's threatened Medicaid cutbacks.

First thing the next morning I called my client, the association CEO, and asked whether he would contact the Bayless family directly. Would they and Alex appear at a press conference to share their story? They agreed, without hesitation.

Two days later we invited state and regional newpaper, broadcast, and wire service reporters to a conference room a block from the statehouse. We needed their coverage to reach our ultimate target audience—the state's voters and the legislative committees that held its purse strings.

Our buy-in objective was crystal clear: get the legislators to stand firm on their support for rural hospitals and get the governor to back down.

Our strategic story can be summed up this way: the state's hospitals, especially those in rural areas, had provided and would continue to supply the best possible medical care—so long as the state strongly supported them.

Our real-life supporting evidence—the Bayless family—was right there in the room. Reading a statement I had crafted for him the night before, the hospital association CEO introduced them this way:

> Several times this afternoon I have pointed out the extremely high quality of care available at our state's hospitals. To help illustrate that point, we have chosen one example out of thousands and have asked a Lewiston family—the Bayless's—to join us today. C'mon up folks. [They join him at a table in front of the room.] This is Alex Bayless and his Mom and Dad, Joanne and Bob.
>
> A year ago last August, Alex was in a freak accident involving waverunners, those big motorized water skis, on the Snake River near his home. In one horrible moment, Alex's friend Eric's rented waverunner came crashing down on Alex's head, leaving Alex in a coma with pieces of his skull lodged in his brain.
>
> No one knew if Alex would survive. But the care he received at St. Joseph's Regional Medical Center was so successful, that Alex's story was featured last month on the national TV series *Rescue 911*.
>
> [He shows a clip from the program's reenactment of Alex's accident, including his arrival, in a coma, at St. Joseph's.]
>
> That first day at St. Joseph's, Alex underwent two separate and extremely delicate operations performed by neurosurgeon T. William Hill, with the assistance of specially trained nurses and technicians—and, with the unique capability of high-resolution CAT scan equipment recently acquired by St. Joseph's.

Without state support, especially in the form of Medicaid payments, St. Joseph's would not have been able to afford a neurosurgeon like Dr. Hill, specialized training for his team, or the new CAT scan, which provided the ability to literally see inside Alex's injured brain.

Alex remained in a coma for sixteen days, undergoing a series of critical operations and, even after resuming consciousness, suffering a variety of complications, from paralysis to pneumonia to life-threatening infections.

But with the superb care he received from Dr. Hill and his team, and later from St. Joseph's rehabilitation specialists, his recovery was truly remarkable—as you can see. [He gestures toward Alex.]

Last June, Alex graduated with honors from Lewiston High School. He is now a freshman at Lewis-Clark State College, leaning toward a major in business. He has resumed weight lifting and is considering golf as his next sport.

At the conclusion of the CEO's statement, reporters were invited to directly question Alex and his family, which they were eager to do. Alex's father, Bob Bayless, was asked if, during Alex's treatment, he had been concerned about his son's medical bills, which eventually totaled more than $250,000. "His life was our prime concern," responded Bob, "and then you started wondering about it. But it never became a primary fear."

As the family was poor, most of the bill, the hospital association CEO was quick to point out, was picked up by Medicaid.

How did this all play out?

That evening, every television station in the state topped its newscast with the Bayless's story. The next morning, state newspapers covered it on their front pages. It was, after all, a real-life story about a local family that directly connected to one of people's biggest concerns: the quality of medical care in their state, especially in case of emergency, and who would pay for it.

Within a week, the governor backed down on his proposed Medicaid cuts and went looking for budget reductions elsewhere.

All Politics Is Personal

As you can see, real life is verifiably powerful. It reaches into hearts and minds, bringing a story message of a positive future credibly alive in a way nothing else can.

That's why political leaders, whose fate depends almost entirely on what they communicate and how effectively they generate buy-in, use real-life examples religiously.

Returning, for a moment, to President George W. Bush: In that January 2002 State of the Union speech, Bush introduced no fewer than a half a dozen real-life people as supporting evidence for his "Three Great Goals for America" strategic story.

Let's "rerun the tape" and see how two of the people were used as supporting evidence (see Exhibit 9-1).

Exhibit 9-1. Real-Life Examples.

TARGETED CHAPTER 1

Targeted Message (Audience's Agenda: Justice and Victory)

We will win this war.

Supporting Evidence

We last met in an hour of shock and suffering. In four short months, our nation has comforted the victims, begun to rebuild New York and the Pentagon, rallied a great coalition, captured, arrested, and rid the world of thousands of terrorists, destroyed Afghanistan's terrorist training camps, saved a people from starvation, and freed a country from brutal oppression.

America and Afghanistan are now allies against terror. We will be partners in rebuilding that country, and this evening we welcome [gesturing] the distinguished interim leader of a liberated Afghanistan: Chairman Hamid Karzai.

The last time we met in this chamber, the mothers and daughters of Afghanistan were captives in their homes, forbidden from working or going to school. Today, women are free, and are part of Afghanistan's new government. **And we welcome [gesturing] the new minister of women's affairs, Doctor Sima Samar.**

And there they were, halfway around the planet from their homeland, painstakingly placed in Bush's audience by his communication staffers. As the President introduced them, each rose before the TV cameras to modestly accept the thunderous applause that greeted them: Hamid Karzai, a scholar on Gandhi, a lifelong Afghan nationalist now heading a transitional government in the wake of the U.S. defeat of the Taliban, and Sima Samar, a soft-spoken medical doctor and human rights activist who, for years, had defied Taliban death threats, opening schools and clinics for women.

Also introduced that night was Shannon Spain, the young widow of CIA officer Mike Spain, the first American to die fighting Taliban terrorists. "Shannon, I assure you," said the President, "our cause is just and our country will never forget."

Additionally, there was Hermis Moutardier, mother of two, a native Peruvian. Less than a month earlier, as an attendant on American Airlines flight 63 from Paris to Miami, Moutardier had prevented passenger Richard Reeve from detonating an explosive hidden in his shoe.

These people, and others, were positioned as flesh-and-blood supporting evidence that America's new war on terrorism was the real thing and that Bush's "Three Goals for America" agenda fully merited the nation's buy-in.

Let That Be an Example

All of this said, it doesn't take a President, a professional speechwriter, or a communication adviser to find and use real-life examples to help in generating buy-in. You can find them anywhere and everywhere, once you set your mind to it. Truth be told, life is nothing but an example!

Say you're seeking support for an idea or change in your company. Think of a time when your idea, or one like it, worked successfully before.

Perhaps you want to motivate your team. Did last year's winning team get a big bonus? A trip to Hawaii? Theirs would be a story worth telling.

Need buy-in for a product or service? Look at the approach Whirlpool has taken! Rather than fill its salespeoples' brains with impersonal stats and features, the company moves new hires, eight at a time, into a house in Michigan where they have no choice but to live, clean, and cook with Whirlpool appliances over a period of two months.

Sometimes their boss, Whirlpool's training director, shows up at 7 A.M. and demands a hot breakfast, including brewed coffee and pastries.

While residing at the Whirlpool house, according to *Fast Company* magazine, twenty-six-year-old sales candidate Dan Fitzgerald "made a blueberry crisp in the microwave. He never believed that microwaves could make food crispy."

Now, after graduating from the program, which is called "Real Whirled," Fitzgerald is out selling Whirlpool appliances to retailers, sharing "stories about his miraculous blueberry crisp" and his personal experiences with the Catalyst washing machine. Says the now highly-successful sales executive, known company-wide for his personal stories, "it's the quietest washer I've ever used."[1]

THE BEST SUPPORTING EVIDENCE FOR A STORY OR MESSAGE ABOUT THE FUTURE IS A CREDIBLE, REAL-LIFE EXAMPLE FROM YESTERDAY OR TODAY.

PART THREE

Putting the Language to Work

CHAPTER 10

Using the Tools of Buy-In

The ultimate hallmark of world-class champion leaders . . .
is the ability to weave . . . vibrant stories that lead their
organizations into the future.

–Noel Tichy
The Leadership Engine

Through the real-world examples in this book, we've visited executives facing a broad spectrum of buy-in challenges, from retaining a sales force, to rebuilding customer and investor confidence, to motivating an entire nation.

The executives' positions, target audiences, and goals varied significantly. Some faced workplace challenges, others needed buy-in in the marketplace or public arena. But the methodology they applied—the language they spoke—to successful achieve their objectives, was exactly the same.

Strategic Story of a Positive Future

STRATEGIC STORYLINE. THREE TARGETED CHAPTERS WITH SUPPORTING EVIDENCE. CALL-TO-ACTION.

As we've seen, this has long been the language of leading executives. In the best and worst of times, it has worked for them. In today's challenging environment, it will for you, too.

The purpose of these final chapters is to begin putting this leadership technology to work in the buy-in challenges *you* face.

We'll accomplish this in three ways. First, we'll run through a scenario that almost all executives commonly deal with and, in doing so, give you a buy-in "workout." Next, we'll outline personal buy-in exercises specifically for you. Finally, we'll explore questions frequently asked about applying the language of buy-in in the twenty-first-century workplace and marketplace.

Buy-In Scenario: More Budget!

Who among us gets all the budget we want in our companies or organizations? Few executives I know. Generating buy-in from the board, committee, or boss for a bigger budget is a perennial challenge. So, let's work a hypothetical scenario for the purpose of placing your hands on the levers and dials of the language of buy-in.

Let's say you want a 10 percent increase in your current operating budget. There are projects you want to start and people you want to hire. Your company, however, is having a tough year. And the operating board has sent a clear message to you and all other key managers: Don't use this year's budget review to ask for more money unless you can justify it in spades!

I've been there and you probably have, too. Most executives, if they move forward at all, will step before that board with a detailed presentation about (1) why the money is important to them and their department, (2) where they will allocate the funds, and (3) how they will monitor expenses to maintain cost controls.

And, they probably won't get the dollars!

Why? Because, in a bad year, what the board members see in their minds-eye is an unhappy tomorrow, for them and their shareholders. The last thing they want to do is expend more capital and risk making things even worse.

So, what to do? *Change the future the board envisions.*

Remember: We human beings think in stories. A positive future is what all of us want to see. So, let's develop a strategic story that "connects the dots" between the future the *board* wants and the budget *you* want and need.

In doing so, we'll "work out" with the following tools that you can employ, in the future, in *any* buy-in situation:

- The *Developing Your Strategic Story* process we've been examining throughout this book

- A specially designed *Strategic Story Outline Form* to help focus your results

In this exercise, as well as future real-world challenges, the *Strategic Story Outline Form*—once completed—will provide an invaluable way for you to organize the key elements of any strategic story you develop, whether it's to be delivered in spoken or written form.

Let's give it a try.

Goal Setting

DETERMINE YOUR BUY-IN OBJECTIVE

What action do you want your audience to take?

This one's pretty straightforward.

We want the board to approve a 10 percent increase in your budget. One thing to consider, though. When will you need the money? Will you need the whole 10 percent up front to hire the folks and undertake the projects you want? If that's the case, your buy-in objective should reflect that timeframe.

Your Buy-In Objective: *Get the board to approve an immediate 10 percent increase in budget.*

Now, we're ready to develop your buy-in story.

ESTABLISH YOUR STRATEGIC STORYLINE

To generate the action you want, what's the "big picture" or vision of a positive future you want your audience to see?

One thing's for sure. Telling them a story called *"Why I Want a 10-Percent Budget Increase"* is not going to do the trick.

Frankly, this board has little interest in what *you* want. They're having a rough year and what you want is the last thing on their minds. What they and every other target audience do care about is this: *a positive future for them!*

So, your challenge is to make your storyline, or title, something that grabs their attention and previews that promising tomorrow.

How about: *"A Small Budget Increase Will Mean Great Things for Our Future."* As we've seen, there are a million creative ways to frame a bright future.

For the sake of this exercise, let's use this one as your strategic storyline and build the rest of your buy-in story from there.

DEVELOP YOUR STORYLINE IN THREE CHAPTERS THAT TARGET YOUR AUDIENCE'S AGENDA

What are *this* particular audience's needs, wants, and future goals?

What would a story entitled "*A Small Budget Increase Will Mean Great Things for Our Future*" need to project, to address this particular audience's interests? For most corporate boards, the picture is pretty clear: increased revenues, profits, and shareholder value.

Thus, to generate their buy-in, we've got to communicate how the bigger budget *we* want will fulfill *their* agenda.

Can we make a credible case that the extra dollars we want will pay off in increased revenues? In higher profits? In a more valuable company?

Tell you what. If our answer is no, we shouldn't be asking for cash in the first place. Not in a company suffering through lean times.

But assuming we can answer affirmatively, assuming we can credibly show how the projects we'll undertake and the people we'll hire will fulfill the board's agenda for a great future, we've got a terrific strategic story to tell.

And, of course, we'll tell our story entitled "*A Small Budget Increase Will Mean Great Things for Our Future*" in three chapters, each beginning with a key message, targeted to the board's needs, wants, and goals. Stated simply:

1. It will generate new revenues.

2. It will produce higher profits.

3. It will make us a more valuable company.

In fleshing out your story's chapters, you'll need to support each of these targeted messages with credible supporting evidence, showing how the proposed budget increase will payoff in the ways you're asserting.

The best possible evidence would be real-life examples from the present or past. Perhaps a small budget project you've initiated before has resulted in a big payout. Or people you initially hired on a shoestring have turned out to be top performers. Coming up with credible examples along these lines could prove to be a big plus in making your case.

Third Step

CALL YOUR AUDIENCE TO ACTION

Ask for a commitment or first step toward the action you want.

Assuming your strategic story has hit its target, there's little point beating around the bush with this audience. Let's move to the bottom-line.

> Ladies and Gentlemen, I very much look forward to taking your questions, but first let me leave you with the central message that brought me here today: *A Small Budget Increase Will Mean Great Things for Our Future.*
>
> *Therefore, I respectfully request your immediate approval of a ten percent increase in my operating budget so that this great future can become a reality. Thank you.*

You now have the outline of your strategic story for the board:

Strategic storyline

Three targeted chapters with supporting evidence

Call-to-action

Exhibit 10-1 illustrates the key elements of your presentation organized according to the special *Strategic Story Outline Form.*

All that's left for you to do is to "fill in" the evidence that supports your targeted messages, and you're ready to go generate their buy-in.

Exhibit 10-1. Key Elements of Presentation in Strategic Story Outline Form.

Buy-In Objective

Get the board to approve an immediate 10 percent increase in budget

Strategic Storyline

A Small Budget Increase Will Mean Great Things for Our Future

TARGETED CHAPTER 1

Targeted Message (Audience's Agenda: Increased Revenues)

It Will Generate New Revenues.

(Provide Supporting Evidence)

TARGETED CHAPTER 2

Targeted Message (Audience Agenda: Higher Profits)

It Will Produce Higher Profits.

(Provide Supporting Evidence)

TARGETED CHAPTER 3

Targeted Message (Audience Agenda: More Valuable Company)

It Will Make Us a More Valuable Company.

(Provide Supporting Evidence)

CALL-TO-ACTION

I request your immediate approval of a 10 percent budget increase.

CHAPTER 11

Now It's Your Turn!

Everyone lives by selling something.

—Robert Louis Stevenson

Enough hypotheticals. As you've read this book, I'm certain that you've identified innumerable real-life buy-in challenges of your own.

Perhaps they are internal leadership or management challenges. Do you need approval, support or agreement from your board, senior management, or colleagues? Do you want your employees to be more motivated or aligned around team or division objectives?

Perhaps your greatest challenges are outside your organization. Are your customers, clients, or investors acting the way you need them to? What about legislators, regulators, or the media? What kind of buy-in do you require from them?

As you explore your professional universe, you will discover that practically every individual, stakeholder, and constituency with whom you deal is, in one way or another, a bona fide target audience whose buy-in—understanding, commitment, and positive action—*you* need to help you succeed.

Don't wait to capitalize on the lessons in this book.

Start now to focus on the buy-in challenges before you. Design your own exercises around them. Brainstorm your strategic stories utilizing the tools we've been working with—the step-by-step *Developing Your Strategic Story* process and the *Strategic Story Outline Form*—provided in Exhibits 11-1 and 11-2.

Strategic Story of a Positive Future

STRATEGIC STORYLINE. THREE TARGETED CHAPTERS WITH SUPPORTING EVIDENCE. CALL-TO-ACTION.

As with any language, the more you practice the language of buy-in, the more fluent and masterful you will become.

Then, when the timing's right, take your strategic stories out to the workplace and marketplace and let the buy-in begin!

Exhibit 11-1. Developing Your Strategic Story.

DEVELOPING YOUR STRATEGIC STORY

Goal Setting

DETERMINE YOUR BUY-IN OBJECTIVE

What action do you want your audience to take regarding your
idea, proposal, product, service, or organization?

First Step

ESTABLISH YOUR STRATEGIC STORYLINE

To generate the action you want, what is the "big picture"
or vision of a positive future you want your
audience to see?

Second Step

DEVELOP YOUR STORYLINE IN THREE CHAPTERS
THAT TARGET YOUR AUDIENCE'S AGENDA

What are *this* particular audience's needs, wants,
and future goals?
In the future you are projecting, what are the three most
important ways in which *this* audience's agenda will
be fulfilled?

Third Step

CALL YOUR AUDIENCE TO ACTION

Ask for a commitment or first step toward the action you want.

Exhibit 11-2. Strategic Story Outline Form.

Buy-In Objective

> Strategic Storyline

TARGETED CHAPTER 1

Targeted Message:

(Provide Supporting Evidence)

TARGETED CHAPTER 2

Targeted Message:

(Provide Supporting Evidence)

TARGETED CHAPTER 3

Targeted Message:

(Provide Supporting Evidence)

CALL-TO-ACTION

CHAPTER 12

Questions Executives Ask About the Language of Buy-In

Question 1: *Where is the best place to use this "language" of strategic stories?*

In any setting, situation, or format where buy-in is your objective.

I first came to appreciate the power of strategic stories during televised news conferences, interviews, and talk programs during which, as a network correspondent, I regularly questioned high-level politicians, government officials, and corporate executives on difficult or controversial issues.

It became clear to me that certain individuals had a unique ability to deal positively and convincingly with even the toughest grillings. Further, this skill went beyond the usual "spin," which my years in the journalistic trenches had trained me to detect and reject.

I came to see that these masterful influencers (among them

Ronald Reagan, GE's CEO Jack Welch, Senate Majority Leader Howard Baker, Xerox CEO David Kearns, and CNN Founder Ted Turner) approached every audience—whether in presentations to many millions or in one-on-one conversations—with a *story to tell*. It was a story built to generate support by projecting, with substantial evidence, a positive future outcome, regardless of current circumstances.

I went on to discover, through research in diverse areas from religion to politics, from marketing to courtroom law, that strategic storytelling has long been *the central key* to deeply influencing others and moving them into action. I found that those skillful executives who had piqued my interest, were, by instinct or design, speaking an age-old "language" that can be applied to any challenge where other people's buy-in is important.

As with any language, this one can be spoken, written, printed, or expressed in a variety of media and formats. Great advertising, packaging, and promotional materials are perfect examples of strategic storytelling. Through words and images, they promise a positive future if we buy into the products or services involved.

Here's the bottom-line: You can speak it, you can write it, you can picture it, you can even act it out—before a target audience of any nature or size. The central point to keep in mind is that the language of buy-in works by showing people that what *you* want will give them a future *they* want.

Question 2: *How do you find out what a target audience wants for the future—their needs, desires, and goals?*

Ask and listen, very carefully.

As we've discussed, this is what underlies successful advertising, marketing, political, and buy-in campaigns of every stripe. Whether they employ simple personal interviews or sophisticated technologies that read a focus group's brain waves while it is exposed to a product or idea, all use "asking and listening" methodologies to determine what turns people on. Then, they leverage that intelligence to communicate the *right* bright tomorrow to a particular target market or demographic group.

For a leader or manager seeking buy-in inside an organization, this translates into consistently visiting with and listening to people as a strategic discipline, a "best practice." Donald Keough, the former Coca-Cola president we met in Part One of this book, once told me: "Every morning when I was in Atlanta I would go to the coffee shop and sit down at a different table with anybody who happened to be there. By the time I got back to the office I knew two or three things that were happening in the company that led me to make another phone call. People would say, how do you know these things? I ran the business by moving around. You've got to have peripheral hearing."[1]

I also love what the late Mary Kay Ash, founder of Mary Kay Cosmetics and builder of one of America's greatest sales forces said: "Good people managers are likely to listen more than they speak. . . . Perhaps it's why God gave us two ears and only one mouth."

The same principle applies to targeting audiences outside your organization. Whether you're seeking buy-in from customers, regulators, analysts, investors, the media, or the public in general, *find out what matters to them first!*

During the years I taught in MBA programs, students were frequently surprised by my recommendation that they pick up the phone and call corporate recruiters *before* their scheduled job interviews and inquire: *What kind of employee, what specific background, interests, skills, or attitude is your company looking for?*

One of two great things generally happened when they did: They aced the interview and got the job, or they decided they didn't want to work for these companies in the first place!

Whatever your buy-in challenge, the same general strategy applies. Employ every means possible to investigate your target audience. If feasible, approach them, directly. Ask people who know them, or know about them. Buy or use existing research online, in print, or in other media.

Ask and listen, before you do or say anything else. It will have an enormous positive impact on your ability to generate buy-in.

Question 3: *Once you've developed your strategic story, how often should you tell it, and over what time period?*

The key to maximizing the impact of any strategic story is to repeat it as often as possible for as long as possible.

In rebuilding and revitalizing General Electric, for example, Jack Welch waged nothing short of a crusade in driving his "Winningest Company in the World" strategic story into the consciousness of the workplace, marketplace, and investment community.

Said Welch: "whenever I had an idea or message . . . I could never say it enough. I repeated it over and over at every meeting and review for years, until I could almost gag on it. I always felt I had to be over the top" to get hundreds of thousands of people behind an idea.[2]

In doing so, Welch was practicing what political consultants call "message discipline."

Presidential image impresario Michael Deaver explains the simple wisdom of the approach this way: "This business of saying the same thing over and over and over again—which to a lot of Washington insiders and pundits is boring—works! That was what we figured out in the Reagan White House."[3]

Advertising gurus have it figured out, too. Coca-Cola, for instance, has been positioned as "the real thing" among soft drinks for decades. As a result, the very word "Coke" is today among the most recognized *words*, in any language, on the planet.

Whether you're seeking buy-in in the workplace, marketplace, or public arena, the longer and the more frequently you repeat your strategic story, the more likely you are to be successful.

As Winston Churchill said: "If you have an important point to make, don't be subtle. Use a pile driver."

Question 4: *In Chapter 7 you said that the best way out of bad news is to generate buy-in with a strategic story of a positive future. But in some circumstances it seems there's just no good news to deliver. What then?*

Certainly, you can't sugarcoat bad news and still maintain your credibility. When things are bad, they're bad. You've got to be upfront and honest with people.

That said, after acknowledging current realities, the challenge of leadership is to *create* a bright tomorrow—to focus on what can and *will* be done to make the future better.

In every example we've highlighted in this book—from the case of the pharmaceutical CEO whose company was losing its number one product, to the anthrax attacks on Capitol Hill—we've seen leaders who found ways to credibly create and communicate a positive future in the face of difficult, harrowing, even tragic circumstances.

Here's another vivid example.

In the wake of the dot-com crash of 2000–2001, Cisco Systems, the leading Internet equipment maker, laid off thousands of employees at its Silicon Valley headquarters. Many were Cisco "originals," highly trained and talented employees who had helped CEO John Chambers build the company from scratch.

With the layoffs, Chambers feared that he would not only lose, forever, many of the best and brightest people in his industry, but might irreversibly damage the fine corporate reputation he'd spent years building.

In making the announcement, Chambers was straight about the bad news: There simply wasn't enough business, or prospective business, to support the current payroll.

Then, he communicated a remarkable story of a positive future: Employees who signed up to contribute twelve months of their time and technological skills to charities and other non-profits in the area, would receive one-third of their base salary plus full benefits from Cisco during that year!

The overwhelmingly positive response to this unusual proposition helped Chambers to build—rather than lose—the good will he had previously created for Cisco in the marketplace and community. In the workplace, Chambers strengthened his connection with employees he retained as well as those he might want to rehire when business improved.

Without denying the downside, Chambers created and communicated a brighter tomorrow and generated an enormous amount of buy-in for himself and his company.

Question 5: *If your strategic story is not working as well as you'd like in generating buy-in from a target audience, what should you do?*

Here's a quick analogy to help address this.

Aboard old time sailing ships, near the bottom of each mast, was a small wooden handle called a "trimtab." By slightly turning each trimtab, sailors were able to adjust the rigging and sails for better wind reception and, thus, significantly improve control over their ship's speed and direction. The same principle applies today on air and spacecraft, where computerized trimtabs enhance pilot control of in-flight speed and trajectory.

Think of each key element of your strategic story as a trimtab: Strategic Storyline, Three Targeted Chapters with Supporting Evidence, Call-to-Action.

If your strategic story is not producing the buy-in objective you want with a particular target audience, or not producing it quickly enough, one or more of your trimtabs may need adjustment.

Go back and review your strategy, especially your research on this key question in the second step of the *Developing Your Strategic Story* methodology: *What are this particular audience's needs, wants, and future goals?*

Most of the time, when a strategic story is producing below par results in a leadership, management, marketing, or advertising campaign, it's because target audience research on which the story is based is insufficient, faulty, or outdated.

Keep in mind that people's needs, wants, and goals for the future can and do change quickly. This is why successful political operatives keep polling their target audiences for the very latest information.

To maximize your results in generating buy-in, it's crucial to stay abreast of your target audience's agenda and to adjust your strategic story's trimtabs accordingly.

Question 6: *It's clear that the strategic story methodology is extremely effective in generating buy-in. But it sounds like it might be quite a personal challenge, and a time consuming one, to truly master it. Would you agree?*

Communication is a contact sport. As with a new golf or tennis strategy, for example, mastering the "language of buy-in" requires an upfront investment of time and attention in order to adjust your thinking and behavioral "muscles."

But thereafter, according to the vast majority of executives I've coached, using the strategic story methodology becomes natural and instinctive. It grows on you. And, as your "fluency" increases, you find yourself producing greater buy-in results in far less time and with much less effort.

One of our Center's clients, the executive vice president of a leading global automobile company, wrote me that mastering the use of strategic stories has, for him, proven *"helpful beyond expectations. It helps my thinking as much as my speaking."*

Another executive, the market development manager for a Fortune 100 pharmaceutical firm, wrote that, over time, he's found the methodology increasingly *"simple to remember and powerful to use . . . logical and easy to translate to any communication."*

Not long ago, a U.S. Navy captain attended one of our advanced management workshops. He had just been assigned as commanding officer of a major military installation where he had uncovered serious morale and operational problems. Initially, during our time together, he wrestled with the strategic story methodology. What should his storyline be? What messages did he need to deliver to the troops? How could he generate the kind of support, commitment, and action he needed to turn things around?

Two months later I got an e-mail from him with just seven bold-faced, capitalized words:

MARK: THIS STRATEGIC STORY STUFF REALLY WORKS!

It may require a little elbow grease at first. But mastering the language of buy-in will provide you an enormous return on your investment.

Notes

Introduction

1. Bill Stavropoulos, personal interview in Midland, Mich., June 2000.

Chapter 2

1. Jimmy Carter, Oval Office speech, July 15, 1979.

2. Ronald Reagan, first Inaugural Address, January 20, 1981.

3. Ronald Reagan, Farewell Address, January 11, 1989.

4. Noel Tichy, *Leadership Engine* (New York: Harper-Business, 1997).

5. Jack Welch, *Jack: Straight from the Gut* (New York: Warner Books, 2001).

6. Howard Gardner, *Leading Minds* (New York: Basic Books, 1995).

7. Adolf Hitler, *Mein Kampf*, 1939.

8. Franklin D. Roosevelt, Presidential Broadcast, July 28, 1943.

9. Winston Churchill, in Tichy, *Leadership Engine*.

Chapter 3

1. Andrew Robertson, quoted in *New York Times*, July 24, 2001.

2. Ken Sacharin, *Attention!* (New York: John Wiley & Sons, 2001).

3. Kevin Roberts, discussion at Toyota, Torrance, Calif., July 2000.

4. Antonio Damasio, quoted in *New York Times Magazine*, May 7, 2000.

5. Donald Caine, quoted by Kevin Roberts in discussion at Toyota.

6. Annette Simmons, *The Story Factor* (Cambridge: Perseus Publishing, 2000).

7. Donald Keough, personal interview in New York, July 1996.

Chapter 5

1. Plato, *The Republic*.

2. Thomas E. White, quoted in *The New York Times*, September 5, 2001.

3. Michael Quinlan, personal interview in Oakbrook, Illinois, August 1996.

4. Donald Keough, personal interview.

5. William Shakespeare, *As You Like It*.

Chapter 6

1. *Parade Magazine*, October 6, 2002.

Chapter 7

1. *Associated Press*, November 24, 1994.

2. *Time Magazine*, December 29, 1997.

3. Ibid.

4. John Sidgmore, statement before U.S. Senate Commerce Committee, July 30, 2002.

Chapter 8

1. Gallup Poll, *Gallup News Services*, September 24, 2001.
2. William E. Leuchtenburg in *News & Observer*, Raleigh, N.C., October 21, 2002.
3. *New York Times*, October 12, 2002.
4. *New York Times*, January 30, 2002.

Chapter 9

1. *Fast Company*, December 1999.

Chapter 12

1. Donald Keough, personal interview.
2. Jack Welch, *Jack: Straight from the Gut.*
3. Bill Keller in *New York Times Magazine,* January 26, 2003.

Glossary

Buy-In Understanding, commitment, and action from others in support of a person, idea, proposal, product, service, or organization.

Buy-In Objective The specific action(s) desired from a target audience in support of a person, idea, product, service, or organization.

Rule of Three A strategic methodology that stresses communicating in threes for the purpose of enhancing target audience reception, retention, and recall. Also known as the "trilogy of persuasion."

Strategic Story A story or scenario that is strategically designed to project a positive future for a particular target audience.

Strategic Storyline The central message, title, and theme of a strategic story. Its purpose is to communicate in "big picture" terms what the strategic story is about.

Supporting Evidence Credible evidence supporting the veracity of a targeted message.

Target Audience A particular individual or group whose buy-in is desired.

Target Audience Agenda   The needs, wants, and future goals of a target audience.

Targeted Chapter   A projection of a future in which a target audience's specific needs, wants, and goals are fulfilled. A targeted chapter begins with a targeted message, or assertion, that a target audience's agenda for the future will be fulfilled, then goes on to provide credible supporting evidence that this assertion is true.

Targeted Message   An assertion that a target audience's needs, wants, and future goals will be fulfilled.

Index

About the Author

and

the Center for Leadership Communication

Mark Walton's real-world expertise in the field of leadership and management communication has been refined over an executive career of more than thirty years at the very highest levels of business, government, and the media.

In 1992, he founded the Center for Leadership Communication, a center for the study and practice of ways in which leaders and leading organizations communicate to achieve their strategic objectives in the workplace, marketplace, and public arena.

Based on the east coast near the University of North Carolina in Chapel Hill, and on the west coast near the Naval Post-Graduate School in Monterey, California, the Center provides strategic consulting and executive education workshops to leaders, managers, and sales/marketing executives at many of the world's most admired organizations. Among them are the Dow Chemical Company, Duke Energy Corporation, General Electric, GlaxoSmithKline, NASA, Toyota Motor Sales U.S.A., and the United States Navy and Marine Corps.

In addition to heading up the Center, as its Chairman and CEO, and leading programs for key clients, Mark speaks frequently at management conferences and retreats, teaches on the Advanced Management faculty at the Kenan-Flagler Graduate Business School at UNC, and is Professor of Leadership in the U.S. Navy's Advanced Management program.

In the 1980s, Mark was one of the most visible and respected reporters and anchormen in network news. As CNN's first Chief White House Correspondent, and later as CNN Senior Correspondent, he received many of broadcast journalism's top honors, including the National Headliner Award, The Ohio State Award, and the coveted Peabody award, for his role in CNN's live coverage from Moscow of the fall of communism.

During the Vietnam era, Mark served as media advisor and spokesman for the Secretary of the Navy and the Chief of Naval Operations at the Pentagon in Washington, D.C.

Mark can be reached by e-mail at *leadershipcenter@mind spring.com*.

More information on the Center for Leadership Communication and its programs for executives is available at *www.leader communication.com*.

Printed in the United States
53403LVS00007B/179

9 780814 409053